New Directions for Teaching and Learning

Catherine M. Wehlburg
Editor-in-Chief

Enhancing Teaching and Learning Through Collaborative Structures

Jeffrey L. Bernstein
Brooke A. Flinders
Editors

Number 148 • Winter 2016
Jossey-Bass
San Francisco

Enhancing Teaching and Learning Through Collaborative Structures
Jeffrey L. Bernstein, Brooke A. Flinders (eds.)
New Directions for Teaching and Learning, no. 148
Editor-in-Chief: *Catherine M. Wehlburg,*

NEW DIRECTIONS FOR TEACHING AND LEARNING, (Print ISSN: 0271-0633; Online ISSN: 1536-0768), is published quarterly by Wi Subscription Services, Inc., a Wiley Company, 111 River St., Hoboken, NJ 07030-5774 USA.
Postmaster: Send all address changes to *NEW DIRECTIONS FOR TEACHING AND LEARNING*, John Wiley & Sons Inc., C/O The Sheri Press, PO Box 465, Hanover, PA 17331 USA.

Information for subscribers
New Directions for Teaching and Learning is published in 4 issues per year. Institutional subscription prices for 2017 are:
Print & Online: US$454 (US), US$507 (Canada & Mexico), US$554 (Rest of World), €359 (Europe), £284 (UK). Prices are ex sive of tax. Asia-Pacific GST, Canadian GST/HST and European VAT will be applied at the appropriate rates. For more information current tax rates, please go to www.wileyonlinelibrary.com/tax-vat. The price includes online access to the current and all online ba files to January 1st 2013, where available. For other pricing options, including access information and terms and conditions, please www.wileyonlinelibrary.com/access.

Delivery Terms and Legal Title
Where the subscription price includes print issues and delivery is to the recipient's address, delivery terms are **Delivered at Place (DA** the recipient is responsible for paying any import duty or taxes. Title to all issues transfers FOB our shipping point, freight prepaid. We endeavour to fulfill claims for missing or damaged copies within six months of publication, within our reasonable discretion and sub to availability.

Back issues: Single issues from current and recent volumes are available at the current single issue price from cs-journals@wiley.com

Publisher: *NEW DIRECTIONS FOR TEACHING AND LEARNING* is published by Wiley Periodicals, Inc., 350 Main St., Malden, MA 02 5020.

Journal Customer Services: For ordering information, claims and any enquiry concerning your journal subscription please g www.wileycustomerhelp.com/ask or contact your nearest office.
Americas: Email: cs-journals@wiley.com; Tel: +1 781 388 8598 or +1 800 835 6770 (toll free in the USA & Canada).
Europe, Middle East and Africa: Email: cs-journals@wiley.com; Tel: +44 (0) 1865 778315.
Asia Pacific: Email: cs-journals@wiley.com; Tel: +65 6511 8000.
Japan: For Japanese speaking support, Email: cs-japan@wiley.com.
Visit our Online Customer Help available in 7 languages at www.wileycustomerhelp.com/ask

Production Editor: Poornita Jugran (email: pjugran@wiley.com).

Wiley's Corporate Citizenship initiative seeks to address the environmental, social, economic, and ethical challenges faced in our b ness and which are important to our diverse stakeholder groups. Since launching the initiative, we have focused on sharing our con with those in need, enhancing community philanthropy, reducing our carbon impact, creating global guidelines and best practices paper use, establishing a vendor code of ethics, and engaging our colleagues and other stakeholders in our efforts. Follow our progre www.wiley.com/go/citizenship

View this journal online at wileyonlinelibrary.com/journal/tl

Wiley is a founding member of the UN-backed HINARI, AGORA, and OARE initiatives. They are now collectively known as Research4 making online scientific content available free or at nominal cost to researchers in developing countries. Please visit Wiley's Content Ac - Corporate Citizenship site: http://www.wiley.com/WileyCDA/Section/id-390082.html

Printed in the USA by The Sheridan Group.

Address for Editorial Correspondence: Editor-in-chief, Catherine M. Wehlburg, *NEW DIRECTIONS FOR TEACHING AND LEARN* Email: c.wehlburg@tcu.edu

Abstracting and Indexing Services
The Journal is indexed by Academic Search Alumni Edition (EBSCO Publishing); ERA: Educational Research Abstracts Online (T ERIC: Educational Resources Information Center (CSC); Higher Education Abstracts (Claremont Graduate University); SCO (Elsevier).

Cover design: Wiley
Cover Images: © Lava 4 images | Shutterstock

For submission instructions, subscription and all other information visit:
wileyonlinelibrary.com/journal/tl

From the Series Editor

About This Publication

Since 1980, New Directions for Teaching and Learning (NDTL) has brought a unique blend of theory, research, and practice to leaders in postsecondary education. NDTL sourcebooks strive not only for solid substance but also for timeliness, compactness, and accessibility.

The series has four goals: to inform readers about current and future directions in teaching and learning in postsecondary education, to illuminate the context that shapes these new directions, to illustrate these new directions through examples from real settings and to propose ways in which these new directions can be incorporated into still other settings.

This publication reflects the view that teaching deserves respect as a high form of scholarship. We believe that significant scholarship is conducted not only by researchers who report results of empirical investigations but also by practitioners who share disciplinary reflections about teaching. Contributors to NDTL approach questions of teaching and learning as seriously as they approach substantive questions in their own disciplines, and they deal not only with pedagogical issues but also with the intellectual and social context in which these issues arise. Authors deal on the one hand with theory and research and on the other with practice, and they translate from research and theory to practice and back again.

About This Volume

In this volume, Jeffrey L. Bernstein and Brooke A. Flinders discuss ways to consider the collaborative structures within education that allow for shared contributions to teaching and learning. The authors contend that teachers are at their most effective when they work within a community. They discuss the need for practitioners to view teaching and learning as truly communal work, regardless of the type of setting. When educators work within a collaborative structure toward improving teaching and learning, they can enhance the experiences for all students. This volume explores multiple perspectives on collaborative structures in teaching and learning.

Catherine Wehlburg
Editor-in-Chief

Catherine M. Wehlburg is the associate provost for institutional effectiveness at Texas Christian University.

Contents

Introduction 7
Jeffrey L. Bernstein, Brooke A. Flinders

1. Learning in the Company of Others: Students and Teachers Collaborating to Support Wonder, Unease, and Understanding 15
Richard A. Gale
Embracing a shared vision of truly collaborative learning and teaching practice provides students and faculty alike with a richer understanding of the value and potential of working together. Refining roles and expectations allows students to build confidence through disequilibrium and discourse, if we are willing to embrace the risk inherent in these revised collaborative roles.

2. How Students, Collaborating as Peer Mentors, Enabled an Audacious Group-Based Project 25
Jeffrey L. Bernstein, Andrew P. Abad, Benjamin C. Bower, Sara E. Box, Hailey L. Huckestein, Steven M. Mikulic, Brian F. Walsh
The presence of peer mentors enabled a complex project to be implemented in a Campaigns and Elections class, and helped the professor develop a sustainable model that could be used in future iterations of the course.

3. The Development of a High-Impact Structure: Collaboration in a Service-Learning Program 39
Brooke A. Flinders, Matthew Dameron, Katherine Kava
The high-impact educational practices, recommended by the Association of American Colleges and Universities, are embedded in an undergraduate service-learning program and leadership team design.

4. Collaborative Structures in a Graduate Program 51
Robyn Otty, Lauren Milton
Collaboration that extends beyond an individual course creates community, continuity, and leadership opportunities for students in a graduate program.

5. Exploring Academia: Professionalization and Undergraduate Collaboration 65
Ellen G. Galantucci, Erin Marie-Sergison Krcatovich
An undergraduate experience working on a scholarship of teaching and learning project with a professor can have a positive impact on the career development of graduate students (and future faculty).

6. Collaborating in Dialogue for an Optimal Leadership Education 75
Carmen Werder, Joseph Garcia, Jamie Bush, Caroline Dallstream
Leadership education at Western Washington University is examined through four different lenses, each revealing important lessons for how leaders are made or revealed, and the role they play in facilitating dialogue around teaching and learning.

7. Four Positions of Leadership in Planning, Implementing, and Sustaining Faculty Learning Community Programs 85
Milton D. Cox
Faculty Learning Communities (FLCs) provide meaningful opportunities for engagement, collaboration, and development of the scholarship of teaching and learning. This chapter describes new positions of leadership that serve to implement and sustain FLCs.

8. Concluding Comments 97
Jeffrey L. Bernstein, Brooke A. Flinders
Taking stock of the lessons learned in this volume and considering next steps to facilitate future collaboration in the service of teaching and learning incite yet further conversation.

INDEX 103

INTRODUCTION

Teaching and learning are ever changing; increasing technology, more active and experiential learning, and the evolving nature of our student bodies serve as just a few examples. One thing, however, remains unchanged: despite the fact that collaboration is an esteemed practice in higher education, teaching, too often, remains a solitary pursuit.

We are both inspired in our teaching practices, and influenced in our decisions to engage in this scholarship, by Lee Shulman's (1993) classic piece, "Teaching as Community Property: Putting an End to Pedagogical Solitude," in which he decries the traditional model. Shulman describes a familiar situation wherein researchers have a community with whom to discuss their work, and with whom to co-author, whereas teachers, in contrast, work in isolation. Parker (1993) echoes Shulman's view that conversation and community can, and should, play a critical role in improving teaching, both at the individual level and collectively within the academy.

At the most basic level, the incorporation of team-teaching may improve teaching and learning practices within the individual classroom. For example, Little and Hoel (2011) document ways that a team-teaching model in a biology class led to gains in both the cognitive and affective realms for their students; Carpenter, Crawford, and Walden (2007) report similar results for team-teaching in statistics. Anderson and Speck (1998) demonstrate that effective team-teaching helps students experience positive models of debate and respectful disagreement among faculty, whereas Wadkins, Miller, and Wozniak (2006) report that team-teaching provides expanded opportunities for student and faculty interaction. Because there is more than one instructor in the room, they argue, students take the multiple, sometimes-contradictory voices as a signal that there is space in the classroom for their own ideas and contributions (Wadkins, Miller, and Wozniak 2006; see also Leavitt 2006). When interdisciplinary understanding is the goal, Davis (1997), Letterman and Dugan (2004), as well as Wentworth and Davis (2002), herald the benefits of team-teaching models for encouraging students to think effectively in an integrative way.

One common theme in the sources just cited is that team-teaching provides someone with whom to continually converse as the teaching and learning unfolds. This benefit can increase exponentially when we include students as collaborative partners, as Werder and Otis's (2010) edited volume notes. Gray and Halbert (1998) point out that having someone with whom to walk back to the office after class provides a valuable opportunity for reflective practice, an idea echoed by Gutman et al. (2010). Whether the dialogue occurs with a student or a faculty colleague, we believe that teaching and learning improve when we have a chance to go on talking, and when the discussion is kept "alive," even after the doors of our classroom are closed. As exciting as these ideas may be, however, we are interested in broadening this discussion to reach beyond the level of one individual classroom and in speaking more universally about the role of conversation within teaching.

Conversations about teaching are not always easy. As Bass (1999) points out, engaging someone in a discussion about a research problem they are having is generally viewed as an invitation to converse, whereas asking someone about a teaching problem could well be viewed as an accusation. Yet, Bass suggests this only increases the need to do so:

> Changing the status of the *problem* in teaching from terminal remediation to ongoing investigation is precisely what the movement for a scholarship of teaching is all about. How might we make the problematization of teaching a matter of regular communal discourse? (p. 1)

Bass's approach to "problematize" teaching is, as he notes, at the heart of the scholarship of teaching and learning movement. When we view teaching not as something that remains hidden behind closed doors, but rather as something that is communal property (Shulman 1993, 2004), we engage together in the necessary struggle to improve our craft. Only when this happens can we be ready to take seriously the task of establishing teaching as a form of scholarship, as Boyer (1990) advocates, and improve teaching on a grander scale.

We can attest, from personal experience, that minimizing pedagogical solitude makes the task of teaching more fun, more interesting, and often, more effective. As individuals, we can point to conversations with colleagues, and to ongoing mentoring relationships, which have made us better teachers. But, the benefits of, and the need for, pedagogical collaboration run deeper than this. The academy, writ large, has much to gain from these conversations. As Hutchings and Shulman (1999) argue:

> [T]he scholarship of teaching *is* a condition—as yet a mostly absent condition—for excellent teaching. It is the mechanism through which the profession of teaching itself advances, through which teaching can be something other than a seat-of-the-pants operation, with each of us out there making it up as we go. As such, the scholarship of teaching has the potential to serve *all* teachers – and students. (p. 14, emphasis in original)

The scholarship of teaching and learning compels us to invite peer collaboration and review (Hutchings and Shulman 1999) and also advises that teaching should be considered a form of scholarship, similar to Boyer's well-known *scholarship of discovery*. As such, recognizing teaching as a scholarly pursuit requires that we support our claims of effective student learning with evidence that builds upon the work of those who have come before us and that we, in turn, share with those who come along side and behind us. Pedagogical solitude has no place in this realm.

Ten years after Hutchings and Shulman's classic article (1999), Richard Gale (2009) urged us to consider that our work often has contexts both "within and beyond our academic milieu." He noted that each category of inquiry (i.e., disciplinary, programmatic, departmental, and institutional) provides opportunities for collaboration and cooperation (p. 5). Elsewhere, Gale (2008) argues:

> (W)hen we begin talking about levels of influence beyond the individual course, we are opening the door to scholar/scholar collaboration—two or more individuals working on the same question in similar contexts will generate exponentially more powerful results. And when institutions or units embark on a collective inquiry, the impact cannot help but be significant. (p. 5)

The chapters in this volume reflect different ways of engaging in this type of collective inquiry.

In them, we focus on the importance of creating intentional collaborative structures to foster communities of shared contribution (e.g., see Bovill, Cook-Sather, and Felten 2011; Cox 2004; Felten et al. 2013; Nowacek 2011; Werder and Otis 2010). Why structure? Barr and Tagg (1995) suggest that, for those seeking to change the dominant paradigm in higher education,

> [R]restructuring offers the greatest hope for increasing organizational efficiency and effectiveness. Structure is leverage. If you change the structure in which people work, you increase or decrease the leverage applied to their efforts. A change in structure can either increase productivity or change the nature of organizational outcomes. (p. 1)

When we change the structure in which higher education is practiced, we fundamentally make new things possible. Rather than leaving collaboration to chance or striving to collaborate only when particular needs arise, well-designed frameworks can encourage teachers (and students) to come together and to build community without the fear of being criticized or singled out. By creating cultures that not only expect but also facilitate and encourage collaboration, we can minimize the isolation that seems inherent in the faculty role.

We argue that teachers are most effective when they practice in communities, in whatever form these communities may take. Such structure requires a level of trust and mutual support, as Palmer (1993) argues,

> The growth of any skill depends heavily on honest dialogue among those who are doing it. Some of us may grow by private trial and error, but our willingness to try and to fail is severely limited when we are not supported by a community that encourages such risks. (p. 1)

Teaching and learning must be viewed as communal work, whether conducted in an individual classroom, with our colleagues at a programmatic level, or even when tackled on a broad, university-wide scale. As with anything worth doing, this work is difficult and brings with it some degree of risk, to borrow from Palmer's formulation. When we partner with others in our teaching and learning, we ensure that we do not face this risk—of discomfort or of failure—alone. It becomes possible to improve the educational experiences of our students, to help them become comfortable with and embrace ambiguity, to model professional behaviors that our students will soon be expected to embody, and to positively impact our graduates, our peers, our campuses, and even our communities at large.

In the chapters of this volume, we offer numerous perspectives on the topic at hand. Each chapter is unique in its setting, details, and story of application, but all are the same in that the central theme of collaboration has moved our collective work along and made it more meaningful to students, to faculty, to disciplines, to communities, to programs, to centers, and to universities, far and wide.

Richard Gale, of Capilano University and formerly of the Carnegie Foundation for the Advancement of Teaching, begins our conversation about collaboration in Chapter 1. Gale provides a rich pedagogical context and challenges us all to push the boundaries of what is possible in teaching and learning. He acknowledges the role that collaboration plays, in general, and insightfully takes his discussion back to student/teacher collaboration as a means of elevating the student role through confidence and trust building, ongoing dialogue, and ultimately agency, which he describes as the "meaning of purpose in education" (Dewey 1997).

In Chapter 2, Jeffrey L. Bernstein and his students at Eastern Michigan University discuss a collaborative-teaching model used in an upper-level

Campaigns and Elections class. Advanced undergraduate students, serving as peer mentors, helped the students taking the class to succeed in a somewhat dynamic course, with many moving parts. The chapter discusses benefits to the students in the class, to the peer mentors, and to Bernstein himself, and ends with a discussion of how this kind of model enabled Bernstein to develop and refine a complex class in a way that would have been impossible if working alone.

In Chapter 3, Brooke A. Flinders and her students from Miami University discuss their three-tiered undergraduate internship program as a collaborative structure in the discipline of nursing. This multilevel approach is an example of how to intentionally incorporate High Impact Practices (Kuh 2008). The chapter highlights lessons learned from the qualitative analysis of student reflections and features contemplations on the collaborative structure, from the undergraduates' and recent graduates' points-of-view.

Chapter 4, by Robyn Otty and Lauren Milton, describes the creation and implementation of the Centralized Service Learning Model (CSLM) at Maryville University, which provides an authentic student learning experience within a professional graduate-level curriculum. Based on Flinders et al.'s (2013) "Partnership Model for Service-Learning Programs," CSLM illustrates the purposeful structure of a single integrated service-learning module within two different courses taught simultaneously. This chapter discusses the expansion of the CSLM into two separate cohorts of students. The authors propose CSLM as an impactful framework for students to think critically and creatively, thus controlling their own learning experiences through a learner-centered teaching context.

In Chapter 5, Ellen G. Galantucci and Erin Marie-Sergison Krcatovich discuss collaborative learning, early in one's education, as preparation for graduate school and even a career in academia. These collaborative opportunities, specifically working as peer teachers and discussion group leaders, emphasize critical thinking, allow for a deeper understanding of academic literature, and provide exposure to the process of peer review. Galantucci and Krcatovich advocate for undergraduate involvement in collaborative structures because of the significant impacts their own experiences had on their confidence and success during the transition to professional lives.

Chapter 6, by Carmen Werder, Joseph Garcia, Jamie Bush, and Caroline Dallstream, from Western Washington University, brings together four diverse voices in describing how their collaboration optimizes an education in leadership. The four—the director of a scholarship of teaching-and-learning dialogue forum, the founding director of a leadership institute who is now a Professor of Management, and two undergraduate students—offer unique perspectives on collaboration. Their narrative demonstrates the value of pairing a curricular experience, based in leadership theory, with a co-curricular experience based on a study of learning. Even more broadly, this chapter points to the urgency of providing structures, which intentionally and explicitly link related dimensions of undergraduate learning.

Milton D. Cox, from Miami University, discusses in Chapter 7 four new leadership positions that serve to investigate, implement, and sustain effective Faculty Learning Community (FLC) Programs in teaching centers and other academic support units at institutions in higher education. He provides a research-based analysis of the outcomes of FLCs, which reveals that they build faculty and staff community and interest in teaching while developing the scholarship of teaching and learning. The new FLC Program leaders serve to establish and maintain successful FLCs before, during, and after their establishment on campus.

In Chapter 8, Jeffrey L. Bernstein and Brooke A. Flinders conclude the volume by synthesizing key points and highlighting the central themes from the chapters. The segment identifies specific next steps that faculty, colleges, and universities can take in order to diffuse the benefits of collaborative structures throughout their institutions.

In various ways, this volume demonstrates that we have much to gain by embracing a fundamental redefinition of teaching and learning in higher education. Taken as a whole, these examples illustrate that the craft of teaching is dramatically improved when we are willing to view our lessons learned as "community property," as Shulman and Palmer, among others, suggested more than two decades ago. Teaching and learning may be further enriched when we think in terms of building and maintaining sustainable structures to house this community property.

Having begun this essay with the wisdom of Lee Shulman, we circle back to his words at the close. A critical theme in Shulman's (1993) essay on pedagogical solitude, and throughout his long, distinguished career, has been the need to return teaching to its well-deserved place of prominence in the academy.

> I now believe that the reason teaching is not more valued in the academy is because the way we treat teaching removes it from the community of scholars. . . . [I]f we wish to see greater recognition and reward attached to teaching, we must change the status of teaching from private to community property. (p. 6)

The more we collaborate with one another, and build organized structures for doing so, the more valued teaching becomes within the community of higher education. We hope this volume will serve as a meaningful contribution to effectuating this sort of change and that it promotes future conversation about higher education's views, values, and rewards for teaching and learning.

Jeffrey L. Bernstein
Brooke A. Flinders

References

Anderson, Rebecca S., and Bruce W. Speck. 1998. "Oh What a Difference a Team Makes: Why Team Teaching Makes a Difference." *Teaching and Teacher Education* 14(7): 671–686.

Barr, Robert B., and John Tagg. 1995. "From Teaching to Learning: A New Paradigm for Undergraduate Education." *Change* 27(6): 12–26.

Bass, Randy. 1999. "The Scholarship of Teaching: What's the Problem?" *Inventio: Creative Thinking About Learning and Teaching* 1(1): 1–10.

Bovill, Catherine, Alison Cook-Sather, and Peter Felten. 2011. "Students as Co-Creators of Teaching Approaches, Course Design, and Curricula: Implications for Academic Developers." *International Journal for Academic Development* 16(2): 133–145.

Boyer, Ernest L. 1990. *Scholarship Reconsidered: Priorities of the Professoriate*. New York: Carnegie Foundation for the Advancement of Teaching.

Carpenter, Dick M. II, Lindy Crawford, and Ron Walden. 2007. "Testing the Efficacy of Team Teaching." *Learning Environments Research* 10(1): 53–65.

Cox, Milton D. 2004. "Introduction to Faculty Learning Communities." In *Building Faculty Learning Communities*, New Directions for Teaching and Learning, no. 97, edited by Milton D. Cox and Laurie Richlin, 5–23. San Francisco: Jossey-Bass.

Davis, James R. 1997. *Interdisciplinary Courses and Team Teaching*. Phoenix: American Council on Education/Oryx Press Series on Higher Education.

Dewey, John. 1997. *Experience and Education*. New York: Touchstone.

Felten, Peter, Julianne Bagg, Michael Bumbry, Jennifer Hill, Karen Hornsby, Maria Pratt, and Saranne Weller. 2013. "A Call for Expanding Inclusive Student Engagement in SoTL." *Teaching and Learning Inquiry* 1(2): 63–74.

Flinders, Brooke A., Louis Nicholson, Allison Carlascio, and Katelyn Gilb. 2013. "The Partnership Model for Service-Learning Programs: A Step-By-Step Approach." *American Journal of Health Sciences* 4(2): 67–77.

Gale, Richard. 2008. "Points without Limits: Individual Inquiry, Collaborative Investigation, and Collective Scholarship." *To Improve the Academy* 26: 39–52.

Gale, Richard. 2009. "Asking Questions that Matter … Asking Questions of Value." *International Journal for the Scholarship of Teaching and Learning* 3(2): Article 3.

Gray, Tara, and Sami Halbert. 1998. "Team Teach with a Student: New Approach to Collaborative Teaching." *College Teaching* 46(4): 150–153.

Gutman, Ellen E., Erin M. Sergison, Chelsea J. Martin, and Jeffrey L. Bernstein. 2010. "Engaging Students as Scholars of Teaching and Learning: The Role of Ownership." In *Engaging Student Voices in the Study of Teaching and Learning*, edited by Carmen Werder and Megan Otis. Sterling, VA: Stylus Press.

Hutchings, Pat, and Lee S. Shulman. 1999. "The Scholarship of Teaching: New Elaborations, New Developments." *Change* 31(5): 10–15.

Kuh, George. 2008. *High-Impact Educational Practices: What They Are, Who Has Access to Them, and Why They Matter*. Washington, D.C.: Association of American Colleges.

Leavitt, Melissa C. 2006. "Team Teaching: Benefits and Challenges." *Speaking of Teaching*, Volume 16. Center for Teaching and Learning, Stanford University.

Letterman, Margaret R., and Kimberly B. Dugan. 2004. "Team Teaching a Cross-Disciplinary Honors Course: Preparation and Development." *College Teaching* 55(2): 76–79.

Little, Amanda, and Anne Hoel. 2011. "Interdisciplinary Team Teaching: An Effective Method to Transform Student Attitudes." *Journal of Effective Teaching* 11(1): 36–44.

Nowacek, Rebecca S. 2011. *Agents of Integration: Understanding Transfer as a Rhetorical Act*. Carbondale: Southern Illinois University Press.

Palmer, Parker J. 1993. "Good Talk about Good Teaching: Improving Teaching through Conversation and Community." *Change* 25(6): 8–13.

Shulman, Lee S. 1993. "Teaching as Community Property: Putting an End to Pedagogical Solitude." *Change* 25(6): 6–7.

Shulman, Lee S. 2004. *Teaching as Community Property: Essays on Higher Education*. San Francisco: Jossey-Bass and Carnegie Foundation for the Advancement of Teaching.

Wadkins, Theresa, Richard L. Miller, and William Wozniak. 2006. "Team Teaching: Student Satisfaction and Performance." *Teaching of Psychology* 22(2): 118–120.

Wentworth, Jay, and James R. Davis. 2002. "Enhancing Interdisciplinarity through Team Teaching." In *Innovations in Interdisciplinary Teaching*, edited by Carolyn Haynes. Westport, CT: Oryx Press.

Werder, Carmen, and Megan Otis, eds. 2010. *Engaging Student Voices in the Study of Teaching and Learning*. Sterling, VA: Stylus Press.

JEFFREY L. BERNSTEIN is Professor of Political Science at Eastern Michigan University. He is a 2005–2006 Carnegie Scholar, and has published numerous articles and book chapters on the scholarship of teaching and learning.

BROOKE A. FLINDERS is Associate Professor of Nursing at Miami University. She incorporates service-learning and the scholarship of teaching and learning in her community-based work with young women, in the field of teen pregnancy prevention.

1

Building collaboration with students into the teaching process brings with it many benefits for learning, but it also requires accepting the risk and unease that comes from redefining the roles of students and teachers.

Learning in the Company of Others: Students and Teachers Collaborating to Support Wonder, Unease, and Understanding

Richard A. Gale

As a community of professionals and scholars, teachers have come to embrace, almost universally, the idea that collaborative practices promote deeper and more integrated learning among students. You would be hard pressed to find an elementary, secondary, or postsecondary environment that promotes solitary over cooperative learning. Indeed, "Collaborative Assignments and Projects" is one of the High Impact Practices (Kuh 2008) proven to improve student retention and engagement. At the core of this practice is the idea that students benefit from learning in the company of others, listening seriously to their insights, and taking into account their varied backgrounds and experiences. And because we believe in this pedagogical approach, we create support structures and frameworks to make it possible.

The same attitude can and should be applied to the work of teachers. Now more than ever before, teachers and schools, departments and institutions, and systems and communities are embracing the value of collaborative structures in support of teaching, learning, and collective development. From group mentorship to faculty learning communities, from lesson study to the scholarship of teaching and learning, teachers the world over have found that learning in the company of others provides the rigorous engagement, creative provocation, and critical perspective that leads to fulfillment, improvement, and excellence. Lee Shulman (2004a) reminds us, "with teachers, authentic and enduring learning … requires collaboration. When teachers collaborate, they can work together in ways that scaffold and support each other's learning, and in ways that supplement each

Published online in Wiley Online Library (wileyonlinelibrary.com) • DOI: 10.1002/tl.20206

other's knowledge" (p. 515). Shulman also points out that "collaboration is a marriage of insufficiencies, not exclusively 'cooperation' in a particular form of social interaction. There are difficult intellectual and professional challenges that are nearly impossible to accomplish alone but are readily addressed in the company of others" (p. 515).

But what happens when you combine these perspectives, merging the idea of student collaboration, teacher collaboration, and student–teacher collaboration to produce a learning environment that empowers students to see themselves as equal partners in the educational enterprise, as true collaborators in the classroom? Perhaps the "marriage of insufficiencies" that is collaboration among teachers, the grappling of many minds and hands in concert, could lead to new learning opportunities for all participants. The result is undoubtedly something beyond group work and peer learning, beyond the student–teacher experience, and beyond the learning communities of faculty development, requiring a shift in identity and a redefinition of the role of student and teacher. Furthermore, such a step involves a reconsideration of the nature of risk and trust and uncertainty, as well as the need, ultimately, to embrace an unprecedented level of student agency.

Student agency, autonomy, and intentionality are of course among the greater goals of higher education. Our mission statements and student learning outcomes reach far beyond the instrumentality of career preparation and skills development into the realm of formation and transformation. We believe, as a profession, that we are working to help our students develop a clearer sense of themselves and their place in the world, as well as a greater capacity for critical reflection and active participation (even control) in their own destinies. As Maxine Greene (2001) put it, "we are interested in breakthroughs and new beginnings, in the kind of wide-awakeness that allows for wonder and unease and questioning and the pursuit of what is not yet" (p. 44). With this in mind, the opportunities presented by a greater confluence of learning and teaching, a more integrated approach to the student as teacher, are indeed legion and full of potential. So, too, are the prospects for scholarship, wherein faculty, their students, and the students they all teach, investigate the various learning impacts of multilevel collaboration together in an otherwise traditional pedagogical environment. The idea links to a myriad of other research perspectives, ranging from the group brain and collective cognition to student voice and distributed leadership. But at the core, the question of collaboration with and for students as teachers is one of learning, first and foremost.

Group Work and Peer Learning

It is hard to imagine a university course that does not include some kind of collaboration as a key feature of the pedagogical process. At the very least, this includes peer-to-peer conversation and problem solving; most frequently, it takes the form of group work, wherein students share a common objective (often a presentation or project), developed collaboratively.

> Collaborative learning combines two key goals: learning to work and solve problems in the company of others, and sharpening one's own understanding by listening seriously to the insights of others, especially those with different backgrounds and life experiences. Approaches range from study groups within a course, to team-based assignments and writing, to cooperative projects and research. (Kuh 2008, p. 10)

For many disciplines and professions, collaborative learning is the coin of the realm. It would be difficult to conceive of a business program that did not embrace and celebrate the importance of teamwork, a chemistry department that avoided the cultivation of shared investigation and critique, or a theater program that eschewed support of multiple voices contributing to production and performance. But in most of these cases, the goal is the improvement of individual student learning, regardless of whether or not the assessments and outcomes include collective achievements or only solo accomplishment. And rarely do these collaborative structures involve the teacher as anything more than a directing influence, or the students as full partners in the pedagogical process.

Many universities have come to appreciate the importance of peer learning in providing students with an alternative access point for understanding, one that comes from another student. Most often, peer learning takes the form of peer tutoring or cooperative learning.

> Peer tutoring (PT) is characterised by specific role-taking as tutor or tutee, with high focus on curriculum content and usually also on clear procedures for interaction, in which participants receive generic and/or specific training.
>
> Cooperative learning (CL) … is likely to involve the specification of goals, tasks, resources, roles, and rewards by the teacher, who facilitates or more firmly guides the interactive process. (Topping 2005, p 632)

Some of the best work on the structure and efficacy of peer learning has been done in the medical professions, which have embraced the benefits and necessity of peer and near-peer teaching for decades. Among other outcomes, peer learning has been demonstrated to support cognitive development, psychomotor confidence, and client confidence, to name only a few (Secomb 2007). Indeed, education is a profession committed wholeheartedly to the practice of peer learning and its improvement through rigorous scholarly investigation.

But it is the very nature of peer learning that distinguishes it from collaborative teaching. Students who serve as peer teachers are indeed academic, social, and intellectual peers; they generally hold the same standing as those being taught (especially in the undergraduate context), have limited autonomy with regard to content and structure of the material being taught, and are not held accountable for the learning that results from the peer-to-peer interaction. They are assistants in the pedagogical process, augmenting the role of the teacher and supporting the outcomes of the course. Peer learning, in fact, insists on a similar identity for those who are learning and those who are supporting that learning, and the benefits of this practice are often tied explicitly to the correspondence between both roles (even when one of the peers has supplemental knowledge, experience, or training). Suggesting that students take on the role of collaborative teachers assumes at the outset that there will be a change in roles, responsibilities, relationship, and ultimately identity.

Identity, Risk, and Uncertainty

According to Maxine Greene (1973), "nothing could be more antithetical to the attitude of the functioning teachers than … indifference. The importance of what he (sic) does must consciously be defined. He (sic) must become passionately engaged in prompting younger people to take initiatives and to act mindfully" (p. 7). Inherent in this view of the teacher is a clear sense of identity and purpose; it articulates a level of intentionality, significance, consequence, engagement, and responsibility that is distinct from any other profession, any other role. This is something well understood by those responsible for training future primary and secondary school teachers, and the construction of a teaching identity holds a significant place in their literature (Beauchamp and Thomas 2009). For students who choose teaching as a profession, this dynamic process of identity formation becomes an integral part of their learning, preparation, and professional practice. Even students engaged as teaching assistants while pursuing graduate degrees generally engage in teaching with intention, usually in concert with some form of mentorship and training.

The same cannot be said for students who take on the role of collaborator in the teaching processes of a typical undergraduate classroom. Although some may be destined for work as educators, the majority see themselves in other fields, other professions. For these students, taking on the role of teacher involves a significant shift in perspective and the embracing of an identity that is likely both foreign and dangerous. How then can students reconstruct their own classroom identities to enable such a shift from learner of, to purveyor of, information, knowledge, and meaning? The answer lies at the very heart of the teaching enterprise and defines the teacher as learner.

In order for students to see themselves as collaborators, they need to first understand that teaching is a reciprocal process of critical understanding, where teachers facilitate not answers, but questions. This shift is not an easy one, even for teachers. "Learning involves making oneself vulnerable and taking risks, and this is not how teachers often see their role.... When they encourage students to actively explore issues and generate questions, it is almost inevitable that they will encounter questions that they cannot answer—and this can be threatening" (Bransford, Brown, and Cocking 2000, p. 195). But if it is difficult for teachers to acknowledge what they do not know, how much more difficult must it be for students who are taking on the role? Ambiguity and discomfort, uncertainty and constant reassessment are all part of the learning process for students and for teachers. This is a strength, not a weakness. Perhaps the first step is for students to learn how to recognize, understand, appreciate, and even celebrate, the "not knowing" in their teachers, so as to allow themselves to "not know" as well. This is just one of the reasons that student/teacher collaboration needs to be carefully negotiated, guided, and embraced. Students who take on this role need to be aware of the impact it will have on their own learning and the learning of their peers; they need to accept the responsibilities of teaching and learning and contribute fully to the practices such responsibility entails. Additionally, teachers who embark on this journey need to relinquish some of the control so often exercised in the classroom, allowing student/teachers to exercise thoughtful direction and critical variation as they develop a new role and a new level of engagement.

Confidence and Trust

In order to achieve this goal, students must come to terms with the limits of their own knowledge and the challenges of their own learning. After embarking on her own study of students in a teaching role, one scholar (Elmendorf 2006) remarked on a number of key insights into student learning, many of which are particularly useful to consider when preparing students for their role as collaborators. One insight is that students learn differently when they are in the role of teacher, taking more responsibility for the learning process (their own and others') and privileging the act of discovery over finding the right answer. Another is the affective impact of students' cognitive work as teachers, which tends to manifest as a sense of responsibility for the learning of others. Finally, students are able to see and better understand the thinness of their own knowledge. "Typically, students focus on what they know and either remain unaware of the limits of their knowledge (the gaps) or hope they won't be noticed by the professor. But when they teach the subject, they come to see gaps as areas ripe for exploration as they develop an understanding of the topic that will hold up to the rigors of teaching" (Elmendorf, 2006, pp. 38–40). All these insights, and more, contribute to student learning, of course, but they also create a sense of confidence on the part of these young teachers. And that confidence contributes to the trust they must cultivate among their peers.

But there are other features of trust at play in this collaborative scenario, and they are vital to the ultimate goals of this pedagogical experience.

Teachers must trust their students as collaborators, providing them with all the information necessary to succeed, all the training required to perform, and all the responsibility required to contribute to the creation and assessment of the curriculum. This is not a task that can be taken lightly, and it may form the real boundary between actual collaboration and the kind of experiential learning that provides students a defined parcel of pedagogical freedom, a limited sense of autonomy and agency amid the sweeping landscape of predetermined content, curriculum, and critique. Although there will always be aspects of the teaching process that remain unavailable to student/teachers, authentic collaboration requires that students have as much power as possible, including: content choice, curriculum design, pedagogical practice, assessment of learning, and, above all, voice and authority. This is the level of trust that defines collaborative practice.

> In both the emotional and collaborative aspects of learning, the development of trust becomes central. Learners must learn both to trust and to be worthy of trust. If learners are to employ their achievement of the goals of liberal and professional education to take on the responsibilities of leadership in a democratic community and society, their good judgment needs to be exercised in a context of trust and interdependence. (Shulman 2004b, p. 79)

And it is this link, between confidence and trust, trust and interdependence, and interdependence and agency, which may be the most important aspect of student/teacher collaboration.

Teaching, Learning, and Agency

In 1938, John Dewey addressed "the meaning of purpose" in education, saying,

> There is, I think, no point in the philosophy of progressive education which is sounder than its emphasis upon the importance of the participation of the learner in the formation of the purposes which direct his [sic] activities in the learning process, just as there is no defect in traditional education greater than its failure to secure the active cooperation of the pupil in construction of the purposes involved in his [sic] studying. (Dewey 1997, p. 67)

On the one hand, involving students as full participants in the teaching process can be seen in this light as the ultimate intentional act of learning. But learning is never an end in itself. Rather, we learn in order to do, to perform, to accomplish, and above all else to change. Teaching is more than the preparation of an experienced and well-prepared labor force, and learning reaches far beyond content knowledge and cultural literacy.

The meaning of purpose in education is agency; helping our students realize their place and potential in an ever-changing and never-finished environment, society, planet, space, and time. Our job, as teachers, is to facilitate the power of our students to do and be and influence their surroundings as knowledgeable, thoughtful, critical, compassionate, and imaginative participants.

> It may be our interest in imagination, as much as our interest in active learning, that makes us so eager to encourage a sense of agency among those with whom we work. By that I mean consciousness of that power to choose and to act on what is chosen. I mean a willingness to take initiatives, to pose critical questions, to play an authentic part in ongoing dialogues—to embark, whenever opportunity arises, on new beginnings. (Greene 2001, p. 110)

In the classroom, students have the power to choose and act on their choices, pose questions, and play an authentic part in their learning. Or, at least they should. Collaborative student–teachers have not only these powers, but also the power to make these things happen. They can, and should, see agency in every moment, potential in every choice, new beginnings in every question. For them, there is no event horizon, only possibility.

Opportunities for Scholarship

Perhaps one of the most exciting possibilities presented by student/teacher collaboration is that of scholarship; the systematic investigation of student learning. This has been a feature of teaching for millennia, and remains the best, and most compelling, approach to understanding and improving student learning. And there is no doubt that the investigation of student/teacher collaboration has yielded volumes of useful research findings, and might well generate even more inquiry into the link between identity formation and intentional learning, the value of uncertainty in learning design, and the recognition of thin knowledge as a motivator for deep learning.

But the real opportunities for scholarship centered on student/teacher collaboration lie not in students as the subject of research, but as full participants in the research enterprise. Indeed, student collaborators are in the unique position of being true participant observers, a method "in which a researcher takes part in the daily activities, rituals, interactions, and events of a group of people as one of the means of learning the explicit and tacit aspects of their life routines and their culture" (DeWalt and DeWalt 2011, p. 1). This is a somewhat anthropological perspective, but it serves for the kind of pedagogical inquiry suggested above.

> The method of participant observation is a way to collect data in naturalistic settings by ethnographers who observe and/or take part in the common and uncommon activities of the people being studied.... The method of participant observation requires a particular approach to the recording of observations (in field notes), and the perspective that the information collected

> through participation is as critical to social scientific analysis as information from more formal research techniques such as interviewing, structured observation, and the use of questionnaires and formal elicitation techniques. (DeWalt and DeWalt 2011, pp. 2–3)

DeWalt and DeWalt go on to point out that participant observation is "rarely, if ever, the only technique used by a researcher" and it is this idea of triangulation (using multiple data sources in addition to observation) that enables a researcher to make sense of the entire field of experience. Teachers can rarely be authentic and accurate participant observers because of the power differential inherent in their role, but student/teacher collaborators have the unique perspective of insider and outsider, peer and perceiver, engaged member of the class and critical collaborator.

There are, of course, many more issues to be examined with regard to student/teacher collaboration, ranging from the pedagogical to the practice, the ethical to the social. Likewise, there are far greater responsibilities that need to be addressed by the faculty member at the heart of such collaboration, including physical and psychological safety, and the orchestration of complex relationships and power dynamics. Then there are the students themselves, who might have a thing or two to say about the whole idea. But amid all this there is the kernel of possibility, the chance that students and faculty will learn better in company than they do in isolation. As a profession, we tend to believe that many hands make light work, and putting our minds together is the best way to solve a problem. If we really do want to promote wonder, unease, and questioning, with a large helping of autonomy and agency thrown in, then student/teacher collaboration, responsibly executed and carefully observed, is a shared step in the right direction.

References

Beauchamp, Catherine, and Lynn Thomas. 2009. "Understanding Teacher Identity: An Overview of Issues in the Literature and Implications for Teacher Education." *Cambridge Journal of Education* 39(2): 175–189.

Bransford, John D., Ann L. Brown, and Rodney R. Cocking, eds. 2000. *How People Learn: Brain, Mind, Experience, and School*. Washington DC: National Academy Press.

DeWalt, Kathleen Musante, and Billie R. DeWalt. 2011. *Participant Observation: A Guide for Fieldworkers*. Lanham, MD: AltaMira Press.

Dewey, John. 1997. *Experience and Education*. New York: Touchstone.

Elmendorf, Heidi. 2006. "Learning Through Teaching: A New Perspective on Entering a Discipline." *Change: The Magazine of Higher Learning* 38(6): 36–41.

Greene, Maxine. 2001. *Variations on a Blue Guitar: The Lincoln Center Institute Lectures on Aesthetic Education*. New York: Teachers College Press.

Greene, Maxine. 1973. *Teacher as Stranger: Educational Philosophy for the Modern Age*. Belmont, CA: Wadsworth.

Kuh, George D. 2008. *High-Impact Educational Practices: What They Are, Who Has Them, and Why They Matter*. Washington, DC: Association of American Colleges and Universities.

Secomb, Jacinta. 2007. "A Systematic Review of Peer Teaching and Learning in Clinical Education." *Journal of Clinical Nursing* 17(6): 703–716.
Shulman, Lee. 2004a. *The Wisdom of Practice: Essays on Teaching, Learning, and Learning to Teach*. San Francisco: Jossey-Bass.
Shulman, Lee. 2004b. *Teaching as Community Property: Essays on Higher Education*. San Francisco: Jossey-Bass.
Topping, Keith J. 2005. "Trends in Peer Learning." *Educational Psychology* 25(6): 631–645.

Richard A. Gale has worked collaboratively with students in theater, interdisciplinary arts, liberal studies, and critical pedagogy, and is currently Vice President Academic and Provost for Capilano University in North Vancouver, BC. He was the Founding Director of Mount Royal University's Institute for Scholarship of Teaching and Learning, Director of the Carnegie Academy for the Scholarship of Teaching and Learning (CASTL) Higher Education Program, and a Senior Scholar for the Carnegie Foundation for the Advancement of Teaching.

2

We discuss how a professor worked with six students to design and implement a complex teaching strategy for a course, and used the students' assistance to create a sustainable model for future iterations of the course.

How Students, Collaborating as Peer Mentors, Enabled an Audacious Group-Based Project

Jeffrey L. Bernstein, Andrew P. Abad, Benjamin C. Bower, Sara E. Box, Hailey L. Huckestein, Steven M. Mikulic, Brian F. Walsh

Higher education faces no shortage of challenges. To listen to the claims of various authorities, students are failing to learn (Arum and Roksa 2011) or are failing to use their education to address important questions (Deresiewicz 2014). Faculty are prioritizing research to the point of not teaching (Cuban 1999) and the out-of-control growth of an administrative class at our universities is interfering with the ability of the university to improve itself (Ginsberg 2011). Hersh and Merrow (2005) suggest that students and faculty have reached a shared understanding—in exchange for not interfering with the precious lives of research that faculty want to live, students are offered fairly easy (if unengaging) classes by faculty who do not push them too hard. Everyone wins under this arrangement—students get good grades without having to overwork themselves (allowing them to enjoy what Nathan (2005) would term "the college life" of partying and fun), faculty can research and do the things that the profession rewards (raises and competitive job offers accrue to champion researchers rather than master teachers), and money continues to flow into the university's coffers. No wonder, then, that some critics (e.g., Bennett and Wilezol 2013; Selingo 2013) question whether college is truly worth it, given the high costs students pay for this mediocrity.

Critics of higher education paint with a broad brush, of course. Our colleges and universities are nowhere near as bad as their harshest critics would suggest; every day, at every university, engaged students are learning with dedicated faculty and, in the process, transforming their lives. But,

New Directions for Teaching and Learning, no. 148, Winter 2016 © 2016 Wiley Periodicals, Inc.
Published online in Wiley Online Library (wileyonlinelibrary.com) • DOI: 10.1002/tl.20207

sadly, the caricature just painted has more than a grain of truth to it. Anyone who closely follows higher education can notice elements of truth in the preceding paragraph. As six current or recently graduated students and one professor, we all see elements of our own experiences in the description just presented. We also note, however, that we came to be co-authoring this paper based on undergraduate experiences outside the norm —a student-centered faculty member who invited six skilled and highly-engaged students to work with him on a teaching project, and to collaborate on writing up the results. How we got to this point, and how others can get there, is a central part of our narrative.

In this paper, we discuss an audacious course-based project in which undergraduate students, working in teams, were able to do a more significant project in their Campaigns and Elections class than would have been possible acting as individuals. Given the challenges inherent in group work, the student co-authors of this paper worked as *peer mentors*, each embedded in one of the student project groups. The presence of the peer mentors enabled the project groups to function more smoothly, and enabled them to achieve the course goals (on the success of the students in the class achieving significant integrative learning, see Bernstein, Huckestein, and Mikulic 2014). In essence, the collaborative structure we set up for ourselves enabled us to provide a meaningful learning experience for our students, as we ourselves simultaneously benefited from this structure.

We begin this paper by offering an overview of the project, and explaining what we tried to do in the course. We next discuss our theoretical expectations of what the peer mentors might be able to offer the students in the Campaigns and Elections class. Our expectations were met, as we show through a discussion of the experiences of four of the student groups. We then examine the potential benefits that the peer mentors enjoyed as a result of the experience. We conclude by discussing the implications of the work we did here. Given the problems with which we began this paper, we believe (perhaps immodestly) that this experience, if scaled up, can bring about dramatic changes in higher education. We conclude by identifying what has to occur for these changes to take root.

The Campaigns and Elections Course

During the fall semester of 2013 (and continuing the following fall), Professor Bernstein employed six students to serve as peer mentors for his upper-level Campaigns and Elections class at Eastern Michigan University. The peer mentors had taken this class the previous fall semester, when the major class project included group collaboration with students from another university. Having experienced many of the pitfalls of group work (especially given that the group members were not all physically located in the same state), these students were attuned to best practices to facilitate stronger group work. In particular, they understood that as peer mentors, they could provide bridges to the professor, independent sources of expertise for the project, and serve as facilitators for communication efforts. The peer mentors would be embedded, one per group, and charged with performing each of these functions. For this semester, they were paid $150 each, out of Professor Bernstein's research funding. Their presence made this complex classroom project possible.

There were 23 students in the class, who were divided among six potential presidential candidates (the candidates used were actual politicians). The students were told that they were to meet with their "candidate" (who would be played by a faculty colleague of Bernstein's) later in the term and present an oral presentation, followed by a written report, which advised the candidate whether he or she should run for president three years hence, and what strategies each should pursue if he or she did run. As part of the project, the teams would have to (1) create a survey testing out various campaign messages and slogans to see which worked best, overall and across different demographic groups; (2) create three campaign commercials—a bio ad, an issue ad, and an attack ad—and test them in two focus groups; (3) do a presentation to "the candidate"; and (4) prepare a final written document for the candidate.

The amount of work and the variety of tasks necessitated that the students work collaboratively with members of their project groups. Students were given a survey at the start of the semester, inviting them to express preferences regarding the candidates for whom they would like to work (and not like to work!), to identify the useful skills that they brought to the table, and to indicate if there were fellow students in the class with whom they did or did not want to work. Preferences regarding fellow group members were always honored; preferences for candidates were honored to the greatest extent possible. Given the wide range of skills required to do a project like this, we made every effort to make sure that each group included students with a range of skills (such as research skills, talent with video, and comfort with leading focus groups).

From the start, we knew the biggest challenge of this project would be the group work (Burke 2011; Felder and Brent 2001; Fiechtner and Davis 1992). Student complaints about group work are well known; a popular Internet meme reads something like, "At my funeral, I want my project group members to be my pallbearers. This way, they can let me down one last time." If given an extended period of time, each student likely could complete the tasks described here on his or her own; such infinite time, however, does not exist. Furthermore, as instructors, we do a service to our students when we offer them opportunities to hone their skills working collaboratively in groups, particularly with diverse individuals (Caruso and Woolley 2008, Mannix and Neale 2005). After graduation, most people will end up in situations in which they are part of a group that is required to complete tasks, under strict deadlines, with no allowances made for underperformers within the group. The addition of peer mentors to the group supports students as they navigate the potentially difficult terrain, and might even offer opportunities for them to share their group experiences in job interviews after college.

The Role of the Peer Mentor

What role would the peer mentors play? The experience that the peer mentors had when they took the class enabled them to speak—more authoritatively than the professor—to what the groups needed. Although the professor had ideas for the role peer mentors should play, based in part on his previous experiences working with peer mentors (Gutman, Sergison, Martin, and Bernstein 2010), this was just a starting point. The literature advises us that student voices should matter in determining how these collaborative arrangements are set up, and we followed this advice (Bovill, Cook-Sather, and Felten 2011; Manor, Bloch-Shulman, Flannery, and Felten 2010; Mihans II, Long, and Felten 2008). This helped lead us to a series of expectations for what the peer mentors could and should do, described in the following four subsections.

We note at the outset that communication between peer mentor and group varied across the groups. In each case, it began at an early class session, when each group met their mentor for the first time. The campaign groups and peer mentors exchanged contact information so that further meetings outside of class, or even just discussions of the project via e-mail or Facebook, could continue from that point onward. The amount of contact between the groups and the peer mentors varied. All the peer mentors attended the focus groups that the teams ran, and all of them were there at the final presentations that the groups did. Whether the peer mentor attended the practice runs of the presentations or participated in work sessions in which the commercials or messaging surveys were developed, or read and critiqued drafts of the papers, varied, although all peer mentors worked with their groups in at least some of these capacities. Across all groups, the peer mentors were encouraged to initiate contact if they had not heard from the group in a week or so.

The Sounding Board. First, and ideally, the mentor was there as a sober sounding board, a voice that carried some weight but lacked the intimidation (or competition for time) that groups might feel in going back to the professor with every question that arose. Having previously taken the Campaigns and Elections class, and having also experienced the joys and frustrations of group work, the peer mentor was reasonably adept at listening to strategic decisions from the campaign team and offering honest feedback. As political junkies, the peer mentors knew a good deal about how campaigns work (almost always more than the students taking the class), and could tell the students when ideas were good or when they needed improvement. Professor Bernstein encouraged these questions to also come to him, and they did. But, sometimes, it was seen as easier for the students to run ideas past their peers rather than to approach the professor.

Furthermore, Bernstein was fond of saying that the campaign groups needed "room to be stupid"—they needed a space where they could propose ideas that were foolish, ill-conceived, or crazy (what we might call "brainstorming"), and have an experienced person offer feedback, without fearing that *the professor* would think them stupid. Bernstein tried, as we all do, to give students this space; however, as much as he tried to be a supportive guide, he could never completely remove himself from the role of grade-assigning professor. As such, students might feel reluctant to share their unrefined thoughts with him. We all need space to try out ideas that may not be ready for prime time; the peer mentor, ideally, would provide this space.

The Eyes and Ears. The peer mentors, especially those with close contact with their group, also acted as an extra set of eyes and ears for the professor, alerting him in case issues began to crop up within the group. If a group was not communicating, falling behind on an aspect of the project, or just not getting along, the peer mentor could inform the professor before the problem became crippling for the individuals, and for the group. In some cases, students were more likely to talk to other students than to the professor, especially about interpersonal matters. In other cases, the peer mentors may have been privy to more information, perhaps through social media, about how the group was doing, and may have been in a better position to intervene. The peer mentors could try to solve the problems as best as they can as a first measure, and then pass it up the ladder to the professor if their efforts are not successful. Or, if the peer mentors judged the issue to be severe enough, they could immediately alert the professor.

Both the peer mentors and the professor struggled with the issue of how to handle conversations shared by the peer mentor about group performance. On the one hand, the instructor needs to use all the information he has to help the groups work smoothly; on the other hand, it is important not to betray confidences, and not to put the peer mentor, or a complaining student, in the role of the "narc." We generally followed the practice of having the peer mentor listen to the students talk, ask their permission to speak to the professor about the problem, and then have the professor approach the student (or, when needed, the group) in a way that masked the identity of the student or students who had raised the issue. This was an uneasy model; in many ways, we felt as if we were constantly reinventing the wheel in figuring out how to address these kinds of issues. But the benefit of having an accessible person with whom to address these concerns were worth the challenge in figuring out exactly how to handle these complaints.

The Cheerleader. The semester-long campaigns and elections project was hard; we asked a lot of the students, often pushing them to do work significantly outside their comfort zones. Sometimes, the groups needed their peer mentors to offer them encouragement and help them see the way forward. As noted, the fact that the peer mentors had taken the class, and done well, gave them credibility to tell the students that it was possible, that the end was in sight, and to offer all those platitudes that we secretly long to hear, especially when group dynamics were proving challenging. Reflecting on the work of Shulman (2005) and others, we know learning best takes place through disruption and uncertainty, such as when students are challenged in their assumptions, or forced outside their comfort zones. When these difficulties mount, the peer mentor can be the voice of optimism, and hope, for the student groups.

The Cajoler/Nag. An additional role for the peer mentor was that of *cajoler*, or *nag*, for the group. Even in the best-functioning groups, the peer mentor *always* needed to play this role. It is quite natural for students to allow too much time to pass without working on upcoming assignments, especially when no imminent deadlines loom. The peer mentors were asked to never go more than one week without being in contact with their groups; at that point, even a simple "How are things? Do you need anything from me?" e-mail might help the group to focus on the challenges ahead of them. The professor would send these e-mails as well, usually with the same positive tone, unless circumstances dictated that the group needed a firmer push. The more frequent reminders that the peer mentor could offer helped the students to more readily handle the complex nature of this multifaceted assignment.

A Tale of Four Groups

How did these expectations work in practice? In the next subsection, we highlight four of the groups. One group flourished, enabling the peer mentor to play the most-desired role of sounding board and content expert, paying minimal attention to group dynamics. A second group eventually reached this point, although it took a timely intervention from the peer mentor to get them there. Two additional groups, however, struggled mightily, leaving their peer mentors to pick up the pieces. Here, the peer mentors played different, less satisfying, but perhaps more important, roles in ensuring the groups enjoyed a measure of success.

The Group That Worked. For the first semester using this project, group functioning was uneven, to say the least. One group of students, although quite different in personality and ideology, worked especially well during the semester. Their skills complemented each other, as some members were quite good at messaging and strategy, whereas others were good at envisioning and creating ads. The group members got along fabulously, and were able to pick up the slack for one another when life got in the way. Differences in how to devise strategy, what to do with their campaign ads, and how to advise the candidate in the oral presentation, were always resolved amicably and with good cheer.

In this group, the peer mentor's role was largely to be the sounding board. The group set up a Facebook page and invited the peer mentor to participate. Her voice contributed to the discussions that the students had. She was able to respond more quickly to the students—and in more detail—than was the professor, who had multiple groups to monitor, many of which needed more active, frequent, and sometimes urgent interventions. The Facebook group worked well to raise questions and produce nearly instantaneous discussion without requiring the students to be in the same place at the same time.

In the case of this group, the project would have worked just fine without the peer mentor. Her presence here was a bonus to the students, an opportunity for them to be able to do even better work than they otherwise could have. Had this been the norm, the peer mentor experiment would hardly be worth writing about. But, as we will see next, peer mentors often need to play more active roles in ensuring their group's success.

The Peer Mentor Saves the Day. For a second group, the peer mentor was absolutely essential at one crisis point. This group, composed of four students, seemed to be doing reasonably well. The students appeared to be engaged with the material, and the first project was turned in, on time, and near the class median in terms of quality. We would have had no way of knowing there was a problem lurking beneath the surface but not for a conversation between the peer mentor and one of the students, in which the student revealed that she had been carrying most of the load, and that the other students in the group were not doing very much at all. She had been reluctant to say anything to the professor (she didn't want to be *that person*), and the other students (for obvious reasons) had never raised the issue. The peer mentor asked permission to call the professor to discuss this, and the student agreed.

A phone conversation between the peer mentor and the professor led to a plan of action. The professor contacted the student to discuss the situation with her. The professor then reached out to the group as a whole, without explaining why, and checked in on how they were doing. Armed with the information that things were not going well, the professor was persistent and pushed the group members to consider if they were doing their best and reflect on what more they could do. After a few minutes of discussion, the group came to a collective realization that things were not working well; they then devised a new division of labor and plan of attack for future work. Although the group encountered some challenges from that point on, the bulk of the problems were behind them and the students smoothly proceeded to the finish line; in fact, their work significantly improved. The peer mentor was then able to become more of a sounding board and less of a group facilitator.

Imagine what this group would have been like without a peer mentor available to assist. It can be very difficult for students to approach a professor about group problems in the first place. If the student mentor wasn't in the picture, the group could have continued along with an imbalanced workload, with the resentment that it might have engendered, and thus produced a weaker final product. Through the communication and leadership displayed by the peer mentors in these kinds of groups, these problems can be minimized and, in some cases, eliminated. The communication and group management that the mentor facilitated, above and beyond what the professor could do, led to a positive outcome for this group.

The Peer Mentor as Crisis Manager (x2). Inevitably, some groups will bomb. The personalities of group members might clash, the working habits of group members might be different, and their goals for the class might be divergent. In these cases, the peer mentor has a difficult, albeit very important, job to do.

We experienced this situation with two groups. The first featured a strong personality, whose grasp of the course material and quality of work was not as strong as he believed it to be. Another member of the group was a strong student, and a quiet, nonconfrontational person; she wanted to make the group product strong, but was stymied by the loud-mouthed leader and the passivity of the other two members. The group struggled significantly, as the loudest voice in the room usually was not the best person to be dominating. In the second group, one Type-A personality led the charge. His other group members were willing to work, and were capable of doing the work, but it would never be good enough, or timely enough, or perfect enough, for the self-designated leader. This inevitably led to other members of the group being less likely to weigh in, since their contributions were not valued. In both cases, the leaders were not shy about highlighting their (self-perceived) extraordinary contribution, and denigrating the contributions of other group members.

Working on their own (and calling the professor in, as needed), the peer mentors did what they could to rein in the leaders of the groups (by encouraging them to listen to other voices), and to empower the other group members (by letting them know that their work was valuable). Often, this involved talking with group members separately, so as to avoid the challenging conversations that would arise when the whole group got together. Sometimes, the peer mentors mollified group members just by informing them that he or she would let the professor know that they actually were doing the work, despite the protestations of the louder group members. These groups never did thrive but did manage to do decent work and to make it through the presentations smoothly. Their peer mentors deserve credit for helping to make this happen.

Benefits for the Peer Mentors

In each of the cases we highlighted in the preceding subsections, the presence of the peer mentors led to more positive outcomes for the students taking the class, enabling the professor to provide meaningful learning experiences for them. Now, having discussed the different roles peer mentors can play in helping the students, we address the benefits enjoyed by the peer mentors themselves.

First, peer mentors indisputably gained leadership and project management skills. In the "real world," students are thrown into jobs that require teamwork and communication on a daily basis, in virtually all fields. Jobs are about people, and where there are people there is a need for leadership and project management skills. As with most projects, there were ups and downs with which the peer mentor had to deal. When group members clashed on ideas or particular personalities didn't mesh, the peer mentor had to step in and act as a referee. By fine-tuning their leadership ability, the mentors could attempt to keep the group on track. Playing this role provided the mentors with a safe space to hone the skills needed to succeed in their postgraduation world.

Additionally, for the peer mentors, the ability to work closely with a faculty member was a significant benefit. These close relationships facilitate mentoring, which undergraduate students need in order to make the most of their college experiences. The relationships we developed also led to instrumental benefits such as stronger letters of recommendation, as well as useful anecdotes and experiences to highlight in job interviews. For students attending nonelite institutions, the disadvantage they might suffer in applying to the most competitive graduate schools or for the most sought-after jobs can be somewhat mitigated by the stronger letters, and more powerful experiences, they might gain through this kind of working relationship with faculty while they are undergraduates.

Finally, the peer mentors got to try out different experiences—whether running campaigns, managing projects, or delving deep into an academic experience—that they might explore further later in their lives. If their future career paths lead them into teaching, campaign work, or graduate school, they will have this experience as a first taste of what those areas are like. We would not suggest that this semester-long, artificial experience was anything like what people in these professions *really* do on a day-to-day basis. But they do provide a glimpse, which is most assuredly better than nothing.

We end this section with a note of caution. Who are the lucky few that get to become these leaders in the classroom experience? Usually, and in this case as well, these roles are handed out to students who have a positive rapport with the professor, and did well in his or her class. These successful students are presented with an opportunity that others in their academic program may not receive. However, as Felten et al. (2013) note, there is a danger that the selection of students for this type of research project is "inherently disenfranchising" (p. 66) and that the practices by which students are selected are "unintentionally narrowing the range of students who might make valuable contributions to the research" (pp. 66–67). As we admit that more than a little bit of this criticism applies to us, we do note that for a project like this to work, the instructor must work with students he or she knows and trusts, which gives rise to this selection bias. (We also point out that although the description of the six peer mentors as successful students is accurate, it masks a great deal of diversity in the path that led them to be described in this way; not all of them were instant academic successes.) Nevertheless, we must be aware of this concern and strive to overcome the perpetuation of advantage to those already advantaged.

Going Forward—Scaling This Up

As we conclude this story, the future offerings of the Campaigns and Elections class are instructive. The collaborative structure of the peer mentoring arrangement was absolutely necessary when the project began in 2013; the professor would freely admit that he was flying blind into the turbulence of group assignments and needed the peer mentors to come along for the ride and play each of the roles described. Based on the work the peer mentors did, the projects became easier to manage. By 2014, the role of the peer mentor had shrunk considerably, and by the fall of 2015, there were no longer peer mentors used, because the need for them had evaporated.

The main reason this occurred was because the first round of peer mentors did such a good job in helping to develop this course. By pointing out the pitfalls that could occur in the project, the professor was able to change his approach in future iterations. To avoid the free-rider problem within the groups, as described by the peer mentors, the professor instituted smaller individual assignments, which made it harder for a group member to avoid contributing to the team effort. Larger assignments were handed out with timelines, so that students had interim deadlines to hit. The professor highlighted group communication more as the groups began, and made it more of a point to check in with the groups. As we write this at the close of the fall 2015 semester, six of the eight groups that term did remarkably well, and one additional group made it through with relatively little friction. The work the early peer mentors did is a gift that keeps on giving – as they have all graduated and moved on, their legacy remains in a meaningful, engaging project that continues better than it started.

This example shows that meaningful and engaging projects such as the one we outlined are possible, through the magic of collaboration. Moving forward, there may well be more opportunities for students to play peer mentor-type roles in this project, or its future iterations. Although we probably do not need to embed peer mentors within the groups any more, perhaps advanced students can become advisors to the groups as they make up their commercials (possibly in tech-support roles), enabling the students to get even more out of the campaign commercial assignments. More than this, having used collaboration with undergraduates in one instance to help improve the educational product we can offer, it will be easier to return to this model in the future as new ideas for how to teach this class, or other classes, come to mind.

We hope others will benefit from the example we offer here, and find ways for their institutions to support these models. Making it easier for faculty to engage in these activities (such as by offering monetary incentives to faculty employing students in these roles) is one way to do this. For students, the money would help, as might opportunities to earn credit (perhaps through independent study projects) for doing this kind of work. We also follow the example of Werder and Otis (2010) in encouraging faculty to offer opportunities to collaborate on research in teaching and learning, and to listen to the voices of the students in this work. This class is better for the many voices, working individually and collectively, that collaborated in its design and implementation. Following Felten et al. (2013), we also advocate for faculty to involve more diverse groups of students in this kind of work.

This project began with one professor's audacious vision of what a campaign and elections class might look like. Moreover, it began with his goal of improving the college experience for his students, hoping to negate the negative descriptions of learning in college with which this paper began. That vision, he quickly concluded, would be difficult to realize within the constraints of his time, and his ability to successfully lead six groups through the trenches alone. Working with the peer mentors made it possible to do this well the first time; perhaps more importantly, it made it possible to do this in the future, and eventually on his own. This collaborative structure and the capacity building these peer mentors enabled facilitated teaching as well as learning in this ambitious, but ultimately attainable, project.

References

Arum, Richard, and Josipa Roksa. 2011. *Academically Adrift: Limited Learning on College Campuses*. Chicago: University of Chicago Press.

Bennett, William J., and David Wilezol. 2013. *Is College Worth It? A Former United States Secretary of Education and Liberal Arts Graduate Expose the Broken Promise of Higher Education*. Nashville: Thomas Nelson.

Bernstein, Jeffrey L., Hailey L. Huckestein, and Steven M. Mikulic. 2014. "Integrative Learning in a Campaigns and Elections Class." In *Integrative Learning: International Research and Practice*, edited by Daniel Blackshields, James G. R. Cronin, Bettie Higgs, Shane Kilcommins, Marian McCarthy, and Anthony Ryan. New York: Routledge.

Bovill, Catherine, Alison Cook-Sather, and Peter Felten. 2011. "Students as Co-Creators of Teaching Approaches, Course Design, and Curricula: Implications for Academic Developers." *International Journal for Academic Development* 16(2): 133–145.

Burke, Alison. 2011. "Group Work: How to Use Groups Effectively." *The Journal of Effective Teaching* 11(2): 87–95.

Caruso, Heather M., and Anita Williams Woolley. 2008. "Harnessing the Power of Emergent Interdependence to Promote Diverse Team Collaboration." *Diversity and Groups* 11: 245–266.

Cuban, Larry. 1999. *How Scholars Trumped Teachers: Change without Reform in University Curriculum*. New York. Teachers College Press.

Deresiewicz, William. 2014. *Excellent Sheep: The Miseducation of the American Elite and the Way to a Meaningful Life*. New York: Free Press.

Felder, Richard M., and Rebecca Brent. 2001. "Effective Strategies for Cooperative Learning." *Journal of Cooperation & Collaboration in College Teaching* 10(2): 69–75.

Felten, Peter, Julianne Bagg, Michael Bumbry, Jennifer Hill, Karen Hornsby, Maria Pratt, and Saranne Weller. 2013. "A Call for Expanding Inclusive Student Engagement in SoTL." *Teaching and Learning Inquiry* 1(2): 63–74.

Fiechtner, Susan Brown, and Elaine Actis Davis. 1992. "Why Some Groups Fail: A Survey of Students' Experience with Learning Groups." In *Collaborative Learning: A Sourcebook for Higher Education*, edited by Ann S. Goodsell, Michelle R. Maher, Vincent Tinto, and Associates. National Center on Postsecondary Teaching, Learning, and Assessment, Pennsylvania State University.

Ginsberg, Benjamin. 2011. *The Fall of the Faculty: The Rise of the All-Administrative University and Why It Matters*. New York: Oxford University Press.

Gutman, Ellen E., Erin M. Sergison, Chelsea J. Martin, and Jeffrey L. Bernstein. 2010. "Engaging Students as Scholars of Teaching and Learning: The Role of Ownership." In *Engaging Student Voices in the Study of Teaching and Learning*, edited by Carmen Werder and Megan Otis. Sterling, VA: Stylus Press.

Hersh, Richard H., and John Merrow. 2005. *Declining by Degrees: Higher Education at Risk*. New York: Palgrave Macmillan.

Mannix, Elizabeth, and Margaret A. Neale. 2005. "What Differences Make a Difference? The Promise and Reality of Diverse Teams in Organizations." *Psychological Science in the Public Interest* 6(2): 31–55.

Manor, Christopher, Stephen Bloch-Shulman, Kelly Flannery, and Peter Felten. 2010. "Foundations of Student-Faculty Partnerships in the Scholarship of Teaching and Learning: Theoretical and Developmental Considerations." In *Engaging Student Voices in the Study of Teaching and Learning*, edited by Carmen Werder and Megan Otis. Sterling, VA: Stylus Press.

Mihans II, Richard J., Deborah T. Long, and Peter Felten. 2008. "Power and Expertise: Student-Faculty Collaboration in Course Design and the Scholarship of Teaching and Learning." *International Journal for the Scholarship of Teaching and Learning* 2(2): Article 16.

Nathan, Rebekah. 2005. *My Freshman Year: What a Professor Learned by Becoming a Student*. New York: Penguin Books.

Selingo, Jeffrey L. 2013. *College (Un)Bound: The Future of Higher Education and What It Means for Students*. New York: New Harvest/Houghton Mifflin Harcourt.

Shulman, Lee S. 2005. "Pedagogies of Uncertainty." *Liberal Education* 91(2): 18–25.

Werder, Carmen, and Megan Otis, eds. 2010. *Engaging Student Voices in the Study of Teaching and Learning*. Sterling, VA: Stylus Press.

Jeffrey L. Bernstein is Professor of Political Science at Eastern Michigan University. He is a 2005–2006 Carnegie Scholar, and has published numerous articles and book chapters on the scholarship of teaching and learning.

Andrew P. Abad is a student affairs professional and recent Master's graduate of the Manship School of Mass Communication at Louisiana State University. Andrew is an advocate for higher education and student success in the classroom and beyond.

Benjamin C. Bower is a 2014 and 2016 graduate of Eastern Michigan University with a B.S. in Political Science and a M.A. in Communication. He will be lecturing at the university starting in the fall of 2016 in the Department of Communication, Media, and Theatre Arts.

Sara E. Box graduated from Eastern Michigan University, where she studied political science. She is interested in student engagement in learning and in effective teaching.

Hailey L. Huckestein is a graduate of Eastern Michigan University with a degree in political science and history. She currently lives in Charlotte, North Carolina, and plans to continue her work in the political field and in public service.

Steven M. Mikulic graduated from Eastern Michigan University with a degree in political science, and is currently a law student at the College of William & Mary. He hopes to practice commercial law.

Brian F. Walsh graduated from Eastern Michigan University in 2014 with a double major in political science and history. He hopes to attend law school in the near future.

3

This chapter discusses a three-tiered undergraduate service-learning program as a collaborative leadership structure, incorporating high-impact practices.

The Development of a High-Impact Structure: Collaboration in a Service-Learning Program

Brooke A. Flinders, Matthew Dameron, Katherine Kava

In 2005, the Association of American Colleges and Universities (AAC&U) began their national initiative, *Liberal Education and America's Promise* (LEAP), to create a framework for excellence in education (AAC&U 2005). In the same year, AAC&U's President, Carol Geary Schneider, discussed a guide for reform, which highlighted "inquiry across the curriculum, social responsibility and civic engagement, and integrative learning" (Schneider 2005). LEAP provides further details on the organization's identified priorities, focused on these three reformation targets, in the "Essential Learning Outcomes" (AAC&U 2007). As part of the LEAP initiative, George Kuh is credited with classifying 10 high-impact practices (HIPs), which are significantly impactful to students, at specific points in their education (Kuh 2008). Kuh provided evidence of HIP efficacy, through his analysis of data from the National Survey of Student Engagement (NSSE 2007). He found that, not surprisingly, student–faculty interaction is significantly associated with learning communities, service learning, student–faculty research, internships, and senior culminating experiences. So, how do we initiate more interaction? How do we engage students? How do we push them out of their comfort zones and encourage the "good stuff" that happens beyond the classroom? We do so by creating opportunities for collaboration.

Foundational Theories and Review of the Literature

There are many borrowed ideas that have come together to set the stage for our work in developing a high-impact collaborative structure: constructivist theory (Fosnot 1996); active learning principles (Meyers and Jones 1993); experiential learning (Kolb 1984); problem-based learning (Barrows 1985); cooperative learning (Johnson, Johnson, and Johnson

Holubec 1991); service-learning pedagogy (Bringle and Hatcher 1996), and learning community approaches (Cox 2004; Wenger 1998), to name a few. Constructivism makes up the most basic level of our collaborate structure. Applicable components from Fosnot and Perry's (2005) highlights of constructivism include the awareness that disequilibrium and active learning processes lead to learning and that dialogue with others furthers thinking. Concepts from Barr and Tagg's (1995) "Learning Paradigm"—namely, learner-centered concepts—have been incorporated, as well: we have made continual efforts to create space for students to "discover and construct knowledge for themselves" (Barr and Tagg 1995, p 4), both within the classroom and throughout the year-long leadership team experiences we'll address in the following section.

FOCUS Program Design

The FOCUS Program (Program Archive on Sexuality, Health and Adolescence; PASHA 2005), a Teen Pregnancy Prevention (TPP) program, established within a nursing department at Miami University, intentionally set out to combine six of the best-suited HIPs into a collaborative structure. The specific HIPs included in this program are: service-learning, collaborative work, learning communities, undergraduate research, an internship program, and a senior culminating experience. This chapter will examine the "Partnership Model" as a framework for collaboration, through service-learning implementation, and will advocate for student learning communities as a pedagogical approach for both service and scholarship. Finally, we will describe a tiered leadership structure, which can be replicated and implemented in any discipline.

Implementation Efforts. After a few years of implementing service-learning in the most difficult and inefficient ways possible, Flinders set out to find a better way. The first step was to identify an ongoing community partner, so that time and energy would not be wasted each semester just trying to find a "home" for her students, in the form of community placement. In the summer of 2010, in collaboration with a new partner, the community agency-university team was awarded a five-year grant from the U.S. Department of Health and Human Services, Office of Adolescent Health, for replication of an evidence-based TPP program. This program's primary objective was to deliver the FOCUS curriculum (Program Archive on Sexuality, Health and Adolescence 2005) to females, 16 to 19 years old, across four local counties.

Bringle and Hatcher (1996) specify that service learning takes place when students are engaged in organized service that meets a community need; this is a fundamental concept, known as reciprocity. When developing our "Partnership Model for ServiceLearning" (Flinders et al. 2013), we referred to Bittle, Duggleby, and Ellison's (2002) definition of service-learning, which merged ideas from Greenberg (1995); Seifer (1998); and Shah and

Glascoff (1998), to discern the crucial elements of the phenomenon: service must be meaningful, reciprocal, allow for leadership development, and include reflection. A fifth essential element was added to our model: authentic partnership (versus superficial or one-time arrangements), which leads to the possibility of sustainability (Flinders et al. 2013).

The Partnership Model (Flinders et al. 2013) differentiates between a project-based and program-based approach to civic engagement, highlighting step-by-step methods for creating sustainable programming. The model also incorporates the ongoing community agency and university partnerships approach, student learning communities, an "expanded" target population (reaching beyond the population the agency or university serves alone), service-learning pedagogy, and faculty–student scholarly outcomes (Flinders et al. 2013). Finally, it creates (at least some) solutions to the problems that service-learning so infamously generates.

Collaboration within a Required Course. Foundational principles of "communities of practice," noted by Wenger (1998), state that participants must be drawn into a common project, share resources, and maintain trusting relationships. Components of "bounded communities" (Wilson et al. 2004), as a means of promoting active learning and student engagement, were used as a resource for developing a learning community that lives within the boundaries of the classroom constraints. The basic elements of cooperative learning (Johnson, Johnson, and Johnson Holubec 1991) are included in both the orientation process and the implementation of the required service-learning course, which allows students to begin building context for their experience from the start. Because course faculty step back as directors of service and collaborate with students as learning community members and partners, the students become empowered and more deeply engaged.

The required course is structured to provide adequate time for on-campus orientation to the program and a "practice day," which allows students to run through the entire eight-hour curriculum and revise their teaching strategies, with the help of the professor and peers. Over the next four weeks, students teach the FOCUS Program (PASHA 2005), a comprehensive program covering sexually transmitted infection and pregnancy prevention topics, in local high schools. Student teams conclude their experience with an on-campus "wrap up" day, during which they discuss strategies for program improvement for future offerings (taught by incoming classes) and reflect on what they have learned. Students report perceptions of significant impacts in the areas of professional development and personal satisfaction, due to the embedded learning-community approach of their service-learning experience (Flinders 2013).

Collaborative Leadership Structure Outside of the Classroom. Because of our responsibility to successfully implement a quality, federally-funded (and federally-monitored) service-learning program, our desire to conduct a disciplinary study on teen outcomes, and due to the time-limited nature of undergraduate student involvement (they tend to graduate!), a streamlined approach for facilitating a collaborative leadership team became necessary. This leadership team, including undergraduate associates (UAs) and research assistants (RAs), has been involved in each and every aspect of the FOCUS Program. For example, they have contributed to Institutional Review Board applications for our ongoing research, completed literature reviews to inform program implementation, and assisted with the orientation of students and staff. In addition, members of the leadership team have applied for internal and external funding, collaborated on the submission of abstracts and proposals for conference proceedings, presented at peer-reviewed conferences, and have supported both disciplinary and scholarship of teaching and learning (SoTL) research. This team is continually evolving, as new challenges arise. We ensure that there is continuity in the program through the inclusion of both juniors and seniors, and by requiring that RAs first serve as UAs, with the RAs that came before them.

Each semester, the leadership team is made up of three to four RAs and six UAs. The UAs apply through the university's learning center and receive one honors credit and a transcript notation in return for their commitment of 30 hours over the entire semester. Although the university allows for only one credit and transcript notation, we invite our UAs to join us for a second semester (or more) in "lead UA" positions. These students serve as team leaders and as liaisons between UAs and RAs, as needed. About the UA experience, one student said:

> The most rewarding part of being an Undergraduate Associate for FOCUS is that the team that I worked with is very supportive and wants everyone to learn as much as possible and get as many opportunities as they can. No one was ever told that they could not do something or could not be involved in a task. All team members are very supportive and are willing to teach each other about their different positions.

Following their semester-long commitment, UAs are invited to interview for RA positions, which are held during the senior year. The RAs are responsible for selecting, overseeing, and mentoring the junior-level UAs who follow behind them. Because this collaborative structure is consistent from year to year, there is both a system for engaging students and a succession plan that is continually realized.

After RAs serve for a full academic year, in the higher tier of the leadership team, their reflections tend to exhibit deeper meaning and more impressive evidence of their context creation. One RA noted:

> FOCUS was my first introduction to research and it provided a foundation for scholarly data collection and dissemination. I became confident in public speaking and discovered a passion for teaching that I never knew existed. I attribute my success as a new nurse to FOCUS, because of the leadership

and interpersonal skills I developed during my time as a Research Assistant. FOCUS would not have been possible without the group dynamics that existed among the professor, Research Assistants, and Undergraduate Associates. Each member of the group was treated as an equal; this instilled trust and confidence in the group members.

Another RA focused on her positive experience as a team member:

> Working within a multi-tiered system (students, UAs, RAs, etc.) taught me how to work effectively as a team member and as a team leader. The support of each member made it "safe" for me to take risks and bring my ideas forward to the group. It was a great experience and I am a better critical thinker as a result of my participation with FOCUS.

Finally, one RA was able to make connections between these high-impact experiences and transition to practice:

> As I reflect on my time working with the FOCUS program, I realize that it has taught me to be team-oriented, to organize, and even to prioritize as a Registered Nurse. The team approach of the FOCUS program allowed me to teach incoming students while helping my fellow research assistants on the team if they needed help. Overall, the most valuable take away from the entire program was being able to work with a Professor that allowed the FOCUS team to be responsible for their part of the program while still having a team feel. As a FOCUS team member, I felt comfortable in expressing my ideas to the group and that my ideas were valued.

Service-Learning Outcomes

Callister and Hobbins-Garbett (2000) explored impacts of service learning on nursing students and discovered five key impact areas: awareness of unmet community needs, critical thinking, overall satisfaction, feelings of preparedness for practice, and professional development. As a replication and extension of the Callister and Hobbins-Garbett study, students in our required service-learning course and students at the leadership team level were asked to rate their experiences on a 5-point Likert scale in each of the identified impact categories.

All class participants and leadership-team members, participating within the period of full program implementation (2011–2015), were invited to provide feedback on their service-learning experiences. Two hundred fifty-six students (93 percent of those eligible to participate) from the required course, 17 UAs (89 percent), and eight RAs (53 percent) ultimately provided feedback, via a Qualtrics survey with a Likert-scale construction.

Over the course of eight semesters, the modal response for impacts in each question category (awareness of unmet community needs, critical thinking, overall satisfaction, feelings of preparedness for practice, and professional development), every single semester, was "Strongly Agree." The majority of both the students who were required to participate in service-learning (at the classroom level) and the leadership team members who chose to participate in this program (whether UA or RA and whether paid or unpaid) strongly agreed that the undergraduate experience impacted their learning and growth.

Although service-learning is a critical component of our collaborative structure, it is not the only significant facet. Therefore, rating only these five impact areas, known to be associated with service-learning outcomes, would not allow for a thorough exploration of our students' perspectives of their experiences. In order to gain a better understanding of how our collaborative structure impacts student learning, a qualitative aspect of the study was added.

Evaluation of the Leadership Team's High-Impact Practice Experiences

Narrative reflections from our leadership team were collected over six semesters (Fall 2012–Spring 2015), from a total of 18 UAs, 7 RAs, and 3 graduate nurses. The graduate nurses had been practicing as Registered Nurses (RNs) for three years at the time of their open-ended reflections. The total number of sources used in this analysis is 28. Data were collected for this study through UA reflections, which included standard university follow-up questions about the experience. RAs and graduate nurses were simply asked to submit an open-ended reflection to summarize the impacts of their leadership team experiences. They were given no instructions on topics to cover and no requirement for lengths of their summative feedback. Key details on procedures and findings from the NVivo analysis are detailed in "High-Impact Evaluation: Procedures and Results", which is located in the Miami University Scholarly Commons, at: http://hdl.handle.net/2374.MIA/5826.

To summarize, even though leadership team members were not asked, specifically, to reflect on high-impact concepts, these themes are woven throughout each open-ended response. High-impact "categories" were developed using the eight key high-impact elements (Kuh and O'Donnell 2013). These findings broadly suggest that intentional high-impact collaborative structures translate to student-identified high-impact outcomes, particularly in the areas of collaboration, research, personal growth, professional growth, confidence, leadership, and participation in meaningful work (with high expectations) that make a difference.

More specifically, lessons learned from this evaluation include: (1) students gain confidence when involved in HIPs; (2) they benefit from opportunities to take supported risks with "low-stakes"; (3) students thrive when given an opportunity to lead; (4) students can appreciate team work; and

(5) students are "hungry" to apply what they're learning and to see results. Finally, it is clear that in gaining more exposure to our students (outside the traditional walls of the classroom), a collaborative structure allows us to influence students' abilities to discuss their strengths and accomplishments. When we are transparent about our intentions, our pedagogies, and our teaching–learning strategies, students are taught how to communicate their own accomplishments to the "outside" world.

In order to support a learning environment that encompasses such an expansive set of ideals, teachers must openly serve as role models in their educational practices: through their critical thinking, their service, and in their scholarly work. In order to truly impact students, teachers must be approachable and interested in students' challenges and accomplishments. Although some structure provides a successful framework for growth, boundaries for the leadership structure itself must be adjusted and expanded to meet student needs and interests.

Graduate Nurse Reflections. Perhaps even more meaningful than the snapshot of outcomes we can see through our summative data are narrative comments from the students who have gone on to begin their careers. These "student voices" (Werder and Otis 2010) come from nurses looking back at their leadership team experiences after three years of professional practice. Their ideas about deep learning, general gains, personal gains, and practical gains (Kuh and O'Donnell 2013) were collected through open-ended reflections. We asked the original three RAs to look back on their FOCUS leadership team experiences and to consider how their transitions to practice had been impacted. Their responses highlight several key themes, which validate reported lessons learned by all members of the leadership team: experiences with diversity, collaboration, life-long learning, leadership, and confidence.

This first example highlights the graduate's confidence to transfer critical thinking and communication skills, honed as a leadership team member, to his career in a professional setting:

> When I began my career as a graduate nurse at one of the largest hospitals in the country, I quickly realized that the most valuable skills transferred to me during my undergraduate education were not bestowed upon me in a classroom, but were cultivated by the close work I was able to do, through FOCUS, with a diverse group of people. This experience provided true hours of critical consideration in regards to population study, educational theory, orientation/training/application, data collection, inter/intra-professional communication, collaboration and presentation. FOCUS truly exemplifies, to me, what it takes to be an effective life-long learner.

Next, we see how a co-curricular experience can foster teamwork, creativity, and confidence in moving on to a graduate program:

> My first experiences as a research assistant in FOCUS revolved around creativity, teamwork and collaboration among the fellow pioneers of FOCUS. I use creativity and teamwork in everyday life as a staff nurse with my fellow co-workers. Further into the program, my role turned into delegating, leading and teaching. The skill of delegating can be hard for new nurses, but I found that I was able to perfect this skill on the unit. Also, teaching my patients is paramount as an oncology nurse. I have shown my capacity for leading by successfully accepting the role of charge nurse on my unit. Another important facet of FOCUS was integrating research skills, writing and presenting information in professional venues. This will aid me in my future as I delve into a masters program and eventually take on more responsibility.

Finally, this graduate discusses her success during an ambiguous crash course into nursing practice:

> As a nurse, I received two days of orientation and then was on my own, talking with state officials about "Class A" infectious diseases, doing in-depth investigations with clients and families, and managing a potential outbreak situation with minimal supervision in a public health setting. Thankfully, I had spent a year and half working closely with Professor Flinders, who had expressed her confidence in my abilities. I knew that if I was capable of playing an instrumental role in such a large-scale program, I was capable of whatever challenges my new job threw at me. Professor Flinders provided me the tools to meet each new challenge I faced head-on, simply by relying on me to accomplish something and not micromanaging the details. She was always there to back me up or provide me with feedback, but she allowed me to develop skills in the area of supervision and management. Professor Flinders always came alongside us, rather than over us, when we were struggling with something. She was transparent when she didn't know something, and worked as a partner to discover the answer with us.

Final Thoughts: Reflections from Flinders, Senior Author

Kuh and O'Donnell (2013), in the well-known piece "Ensuring Quality and Taking High-Impact Practices to Scale," argue that HIPs should be required, rather than optional. One of LEAP's more recent initiatives is to make excellence inclusive (AAC&U 2014), as HIPs have been found to be particularly effective for underserved students (Finley and McNair 2013). High-impact and collaborative initiatives will only become more prevalent as higher education answers the call to do better by our students. However, student–faculty collaboration, at the level that we describe, and within the context of service and research, takes both a firm commitment and a significant amount of trust on the part of the professor. It requires motivation, dedication, and trust from the students as well. There are so many things out of our control once we leave the safety of our classrooms, and the stakes are high, for both students and professors. For students, grades can suffer and confidence can be shaken if they aren't properly set up to succeed. For professors, relationships with community partners are on the line, the integrity of research processes could be compromised, and presenting with students at professional conferences, when they are given an opportunity to move the presentation in their own directions, can feel very risky. Returning to Fosnot and Perry's (2005) constructivism insights, which created our theoretical underpinnings for this work, we recall that self-organization and active learning push us to learn, dialogue with others furthers ideas, and disequilibrium, which feels uncomfortable, leads to learning—our ultimate goal.

It is difficult to summarize all the lessons that my work in collaborative structures has taught me. My experiences with my students, outside of the classroom, have transformed us all. My students have gained confidence and critical skills in leadership and teamwork that will impact the rest of their careers. My teaching and scholarship will never be the same.

What I do know is that when we create time, space, situations, and opportunities to listen to our students, we can better provide the guidance that they need. By finding some sort of collaborative structure to situate ourselves in as faculty members and as scholars, we can allow our students to find us. They can step up and do more and dig deeper. If we are willing to take chances and talk about our work, with students and colleagues—even if it's not perfect or finished or right—(maybe even *especially* if it's not perfect or finished or right), our teaching and learning outcomes can only improve.

Acknowledgments

This project was supported by Grant Number TP1AH000050-01-01 from the U.S. Department of Health and Human Services, Office of Adolescent Health. The content of this manuscript is solely the responsibility of the authors and does not necessarily represent the official views of the U.S. Department of Health and Human Services.

References

Association of American Colleges and Universities (AAC&U). 2014. *An Introduction to LEAP*. Washington, DC: Association of American Colleges. https://aacu.org/sites/default/files/files/LEAP/Introduction_to_LEAP.pdf

Association of American Colleges and Universities (AAC&U). 2007. *College Learning for the New Global Century: A Report from the National Leadership Council for Liberal Education & America's Promise*. Washington, DC: Association of American Colleges. http://files.eric.ed.gov/fulltext/ED495004.pdf

Association of American Colleges and Universities (AAC&U). 2005. *The Leap Challenge*. Washington, D.C.: Association of American Colleges. https://www.aacu.org/sites/default/files/files/LEAP/LEAPChallengeBrochure.pdf

Barr, Robert B., and John Tagg. 1995. "From Teaching to Learning: A New Paradigm for Undergraduate Education." *Change* 27(6): 12–25.

Barrows, Howard S. 1985. *How to Design a Problem-Based Curriculum for the Preclinical Years*. New York: Springer.

Bittle, Mary, Wendy Duggleby, and Patty Ellison. 2002. "Implementation of the Essential Elements of Service Learning in Three Nursing Courses." *Journal of Nursing Education* 41(3): 129–132.

Bringle, Robert G., and Julie A. Hatcher. 1996. "Implementing Service Learning in Higher Education." *Journal of Higher Education* 67(2): 67–73.

Callister, Lynn Clark, and Debra Hobbins-Garbett. 2000. "Enter to Learn, Go Forth to Serve: Service Learning In Nursing Education." *Journal of Professional Nursing* 16(3): 177–183.

Cox, Milton D. 2004. "Introduction to Faculty Learning Communities." In *Building Faculty Learning Communities*, New Directions for Teaching and Learning, no. 97, edited by Milton D. Cox and Laurie Richlin, 5–23. San Francisco: Jossey-Bass.

Finley, Ashley, and Tia McNair. 2013. *Assessing Underserved Students' Engagement in High-Impact Practices*. Washington, DC: Association of American Colleges.

Flinders, Brooke. 2013. "Service-Learning Pedagogy: Benefits of a Learning Community." *Journal of College Teaching and Learning* 10(3): 159–166.

Flinders, Brooke, Louis Nicholson, Allison Carlascio, and Katelyn Gilb. 2013. "The Partnership Model for Service-Learning Programs: A Step-By-Step Approach." *American Journal of Health Sciences* 4(2): 67–77.

Fosnot, Catherine Twomey, ed. 1996. *Constructivism, Theory, Perspectives and Practice*. New York: Teachers College Press.

Fosnot, Catherine Twomey, and Randall Stewart Perry. 2005. "Constructivism: A Psychological Theory of Learning." In *Constructivism. Theory, Perspectives, and Practice*, 2nd ed., edited by Catherine Twomey Fosnot. New York: Teachers College Press.

Greenberg, Jerrold S. 1995. "Health Care: First the Heart, Then the Head." *Journal of Health Education* 26(4): 214–223.

Johnson, David W., Roger T. Johnson, and Edythe Johnson Holubec. 1991. *Cooperation in the Classroom*. Edina, MN: Interaction Book.

Kolb, David A. 1984. *Experiential Learning: Experience as the Source of Learning and Development*. Englewood Cliffs, NJ: Prentice Hall.

Kuh, George. 2008. *High-Impact Educational Practices: What They Are, Who Has Access to Them, and Why They Matter*. Washington, DC: Association of American Colleges.

Kuh, George, and Ken O'Donnell. 2013. *Ensuring Quality and Taking High-Impact Practices to Scale*. Washington, DC: Association of American Colleges.

Meyers, Chet, and Thomas B. Jones. 1993. *Promoting Active Learning: Strategies for the College Classroom*. San Francisco: Jossey-Bass.

National Survey of Student Engagement. 2007. *Experiences That Matter: Enhancing Student Learning and Success: Annual Report 2007*. Bloomington: Indiana University Center for Postsecondary Research.

Program Archive on Sexuality, Health and Adolescence (PASHA), Sociometrics Corporation. 2005. *FOCUS: Preventing Sexually Transmitted Infections and Unintended Pregnancies Among Young Women*. Los Altos, CA.

Schneider, Carol Geary. 2005. "Making Excellence Inclusive: Liberal Education and America's Promise." *Liberal Education* 91(2). https://www.aacu.org/liberaleducation/2014/fall/schneider-leap

Seifer, Sarena Diane. 1998. "Service-Learning: Community-Campus Partnerships for Health Professions Education." *Academic Medicine* 73(3): 272–277.

Shah, Nina P., and Mary A. Glascoff. 1998. "The Community as Classroom: Service-Learning in Tillery, North Carolina." In *Caring and Community: Concept and Models for Service-Learning in Nursing*, edited by Jane Norbeck, Charlene Connolly, and JoEllen Koerner. Washington, DC: American Association for Higher Education.

Wenger, Etienne. 1998. *Communities of Practice: Learning, Meaning, and Identity*. Cambridge, UK: Cambridge University Press.

Werder, Carmen, and Megan Otis, eds. 2010. *Engaging Student Voices in the Study of Teaching and Learning*. Sterling, VA: Stylus Press.

Wilson, Brent, Stacey Ludwig-Hardman, Christine Thornam, and Joanna C. Dunlap. 2004. "Bounded Community: Designing and Facilitating Learning Communities in Formal Courses." *The International Review of Research in Open and Distance Learning* 5(3): 1–22.

BROOKE A. FLINDERS *is Associate Professor of Nursing at Miami University. She incorporates service-learning and the scholarship of teaching and learning into her community-based work with young women in the field of women's health and teen pregnancy prevention.*

MATTHEW DAMERON *is a 2015 graduate of Miami University's Baccalaureate nursing program. He is a registered nurse, currently practicing in critical care.*

KATHERINE KAVA *is a 2015 graduate of Miami University's Baccalaureate nursing program. She is a registered nurse, currently practicing in neonatal intensive care.*

4

This chapter describes the Centralized Service Learning Model (CSLM), a collaborative-teaching structure that connects two separate courses with one service-learning project. We discuss the lessons learned from applying the CSLM in our courses.

Collaborative Structures in a Graduate Program

Robyn Otty, Lauren Milton

Service learning is widely documented in the literature as an accepted pedagogy in higher education, due to the fulfillment of civic engagement requirements and the limitless learning that encourages a student's ability to think critically (Heinrich et al. 2015), while engaging in real-world issues (Sabo et al. 2015). Although service learning, from an institutional point of view, largely focuses on learning outcomes and student retention, collaborative relationships among faculty, students, and community partners have an added benefit of enriching the contextual learning environment. One successful approach to service learning is collaborative teaching. This approach encourages the element of purposeful interactions to support interpersonal skill development, as expected within the workplace, and creates deeper learning and understanding (Barkley, Major, and Cross 2014). A collaborative approach to teaching can collectively shape the academy's strategic implementation plan to ensure the college experience meets students' intellectual and social needs while providing a service to the community.

Service Learning

The changes in the landscape of higher education are due, in part, to changing expectations of students (Bowen et al. 2011). To produce effective service learning experiences in the community, from the student-centric perspective, faculty should provide a structure to the given experience to facilitate the greatest impact. The literature supports students' appreciation for experiential learning and faculty allowances to learn by doing (Bowen et al. 2011; Pope-Ruark et al. 2014). Despite the changes in the student population, research asserts that students have similar beliefs about learning when compared to faculty and share a desire to

New Directions for Teaching and Learning, no. 148, Winter 2016 © 2016 Wiley Periodicals, Inc.
Published online in Wiley Online Library (wileyonlinelibrary.com) • DOI: 10.1002/tl.20209

learn both within the context of the classroom and beyond (Dandy and Bendersky 2014).

The act of service as a teaching tool provides context and opportunity for faculty and students to interact within the community in positive ways, beyond the boundaries of bricks and mortar (McDonald and Dominguez 2015). In recent years, higher education institutions have included service learning within their strategic institutional culture, often touting hands-on learning opportunities and student engagement as central values to the institution's experience. Even though active learning has been repackaged in higher education as civic or community engagement, service learning provides a legitimate and valid way for "producing and mobilizing knowledge" (Gelmon, Jordan, and Seifer 2013, p. 58).

The increased attention to service learning has been supported in the literature, further strengthening its value in higher education as a respectable mode of pre-work experience. Research supports the effectiveness of service learning as a pedagogical approach to enable greater understanding of the course material through authentic problem solving and engaged activity in the community (Flinders 2013; Sabo et al. 2015). Such learning experiences provide avenues for students to be immersed in situations that require complex decision-making skills, which can be generalized into their lives as productive individuals, thereby increasing employability (Flinders 2013; Levkoe, Brail, and Daniere 2014).

Service learning has also been connected to teaching with the recent emphasis on students' perspectives. In Werder and Otis's (2010) book, *Engaging Student Voices in the Study of Teaching and Learning*, author Kelly Flannery asserts, "Using student voices allows students to actively participate in their education and recognize that other people, in conjunction with the professor, can offer a valuable contribution to the classroom . . . . It enables students to perceive themselves and their classmates as having more power in their education" (Manor et al. 2010, p. 11). Bruton's (2011, p. 35) work regarding student voice also suggests students' self-perceptions of creativity can be expanded: "[L]earning creativity for innovation is possible, by raising awareness of becoming involved in creative ventures, appreciating creative thinking strategies." Additionally, creating opportunities for structured environments that encourage students to apply, discover, analyze, and take risks can enhance problem solving beyond our highly visual culture. Student motivation can also be influenced by the relationship with the community partnership (Pope-Ruark et al. 2014). This internal purpose or "move to action" to meet the needs of the community partner can be encouraged within supported service learning projects (Mbugua and Godek 2012, p. 31). In essence, the community partner's experience, in turn, contributes to students' developed skills, thereby translating the experience into potential future work experiences (Jacobson 2015).

Finally, with the many academic benefits of service learning, the affective and expected real-world professional development of self also can be supported. Yorio and Ye's (2012) meta-analysis found service learning has a significant impact on personal insight and awareness of one's own personal development. Service learning creates autonomy and opportunity for the student to gain greater confidence through the experience of inherent self-doubt, failures, and learning from such to build new positive experiences. In addition, service learning facilitates the social experience among peers collaborating to accomplish their shared goal. These combined benefits of service learning move the student role from a passive recipient to an active agent and creator of new knowledge (Johnson 2014, p. 31).

Collaborative Teaching Approach

In recent years, collaborative teaching as a service learning approach has grown in popularity in higher education. More widely known as co-teaching within K–12 educational systems, collaborative teaching allows two or more teachers who are equal in status to work together with the same students to provide instruction (Blanchard 2012; Bouck 2007). Co-teaching is seen as a highly complex, synergistic relationship in which both teachers negotiate roles within the classroom from instruction to management and discipline (Bouck 2007). Given that more than one teacher shares the expected classroom responsibilities, it affords additional time and freedom for new experiences and supplementary support for unanticipated needs.

In a course designed with a collaborative structure, the learning becomes a shared partnership between instructors, students, community partners, and program participants. Through this intentional connection among stakeholders, collaborative structures naturally incorporate the emotional and social aspects of learning. In addition, within a collaborative learning environment, the teacher moves away from instructor-led lectures, or "sage on the stage" (King 1993, p. 30). Instead, the teacher creates greater student autonomy and learning, thereby reshaping "relationships of teacher-student and student-student" (Osterholt and Barratt 2012, p. 23). Through this pedagogical shift, individual student learning and experiences can encourage critical thinking and enhance emotional intelligence skills that embrace leadership growth. Flinders, Dameron, and Kava's (2016) work includes a leadership component infused within their collaborative structure that incorporates service learning, collaborative assignments, learning communities, undergraduate research, an internship program, and a culminating experience. Several of Flinders et al.'s (2016) student leadership team members report perceptions of improved self-efficacy, interpersonal skills, and confidence through their involvement in an instructor-designed collaborative structure.

Collaborative learning within a group provides opportunities for peer-to-peer discussion and discourse, which reinforce student learning. Curseau and Pluut's (2013, p. 99) study described such student groupings as "learning entities" that allow students to be more prepared for an increasingly diverse workforce after college. Group dynamics and peer-to-peer learning allow students to problem-solve through engaging discussions, thus providing additional opportunities for learning. Such student-directed problem solving, motivation, and creative cooperative strategies can also be further developed and practiced. Therefore, collaborative learning reinforces student learning, creates a strong motivation to learn complex concepts, and most importantly, provides an opportunity to create and make mistakes that traditional pedagogy does not always encourage (Rassuli and Manzer 2005).

Supporting collaborative learning requires intention, thoughtful consideration, and planning. Due to the necessity to build relationships with community partners, while carefully crafting a course to encourage instructor-to-student collaboration, the instructor must not lose sight of the moving parts that make up a collaborative structure. Most impactful collaborative learning occurs when an instructor interacts with students and creates the necessary course structure and management (Curseau and Pluut 2013). Flinders et al.'s (2013) Partnership Model for Service-Learning provides such course structure to support collaborative learning opportunities with engaged groups while combining the instructor's scholarly endeavors with service.

Combining Service Learning and Collaborative Teaching

Service learning and collaborative teaching are often seen in the literature as separate pedagogical concepts. Collaborative teaching serves as a tool rooted in service learning and can be easily incorporated through a collaborative structure. One such structure, the Centralized Service Learning Model (CSLM), purposefully creates a collaborative framework between two faculty members. These colleagues coordinate two different courses and facilitate the work of multiple student groups with one central service-learning project. Through the CSLM, faculty members are able to create a synergistic blending of two different courses with a service-learning experience to enrich the connection with the community partner and foster necessary skills for future employment. The CSLM aims "to enrich the connections between doing and knowing" (Kalles and Ryan 2015, p. 133), while creating opportunities to solve problems and plan within a group.

The CSLM serves the common purpose of helping the community while providing authentic learning experiences outside the confines of a university campus. With the service learning aspects, this model also encourages in-depth learning experiences through connected experiences with faculty and community stakeholders. This chapter will illustrate the process and development of a collaborative structure, the CSLM, describe the students' perspectives, and highlight recommendations for successful implementation.

Figure 4.1. Centralized Service Learning Model: Year One

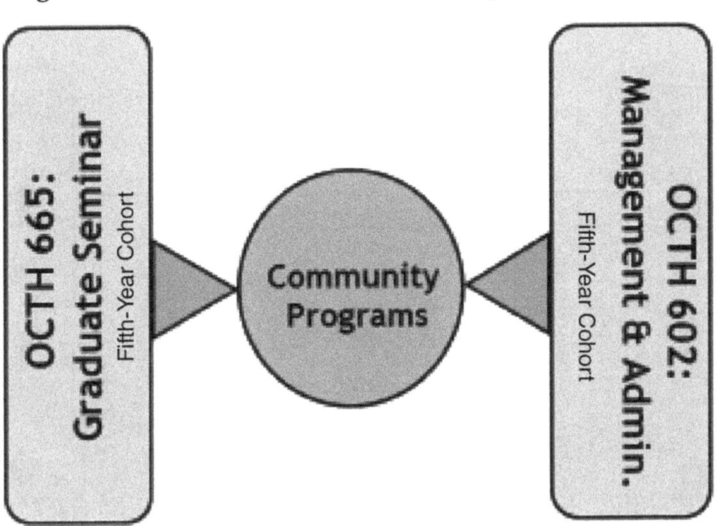

The Centralized Service Learning Model: Development

In October of 2012 at a scholarship of teaching and learning conference, one breakout session featured an innovative model for combining service, teaching, and scholarship: the Partnership Model for Service-Learning (Flinders et al. 2013). From a pedagogical framework, this model presented the benefits of experiential service learning within a real-world context. This logical and highly practical approach to "three birds (scholarship, service, and teaching) and one stone" (faculty member) became the core beginning of the CSLM. The CSLM extends the partnership model for service learning through the embedding of a single service-learning activity within two different courses.

Within an occupational therapy graduate level program, the CSLM was applied during the final semester, as part of a culminating experience. Prior to this semester, the students complete two 12-week-long fieldwork experiences and emerge with the ability to work at the equivalent level of entry-level professionals. Given that those students learn directly in the field for six months as part of their occupational therapy education, two full-time faculty members recognized the opportunity for students to maximize their skills and experiences during the semester back on campus, resulting in the development and launch of CSLM as part of two separate courses, Graduate Seminar and Management & Administration (see Figure 4.1).

The Graduate Seminar is a capstone course that affords students the opportunity to demonstrate achievement of learning objectives established by the OT program. With a faculty mentor, students work in groups to apply

Figure 4.2. CSLM with Associated Student Learning Activities: Year One

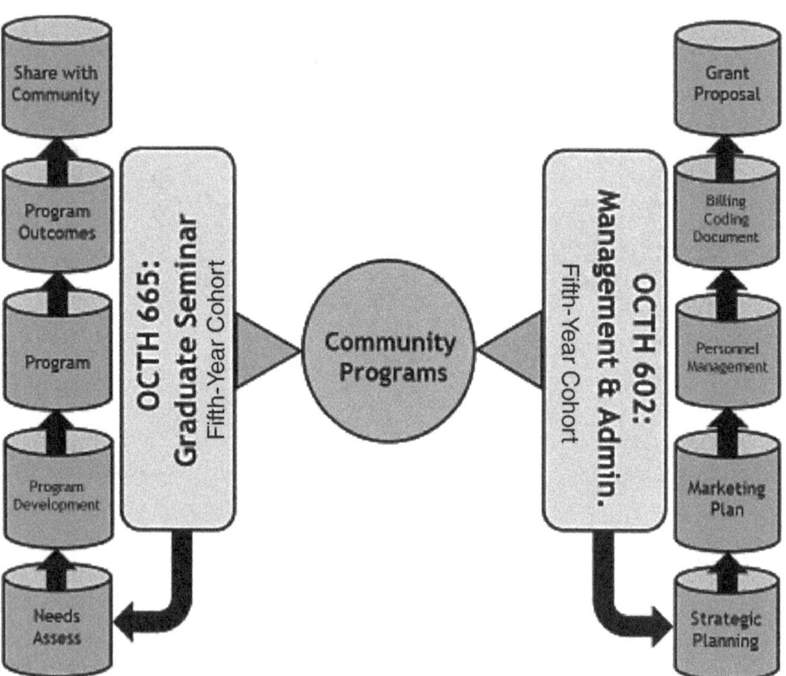

both their newfound clinical skills and program development knowledge acquired within the curriculum to a service learning project that functions as the main evaluation criteria for the course (see Figure 4.2). Student learning activities, such as conducting a needs assessment and developing and implementing a program, build on each other as the semester progresses. Students ultimately engage in the delivery of a report of program outcomes to their community partner. The Management & Administration course occurs concurrently with the Graduate Seminar and allows students to explore facets of healthcare management, including strategic planning; marketing; personnel management; and billing, coding, and documentation. As a culminating activity in Management & Administration, student groups engage in grant writing for their respective program.

Year One—Spring 2013. During year one of implementation, a three-week long, after-school, remedial-based handwriting and fine motor program was planned and implemented by graduate-level occupational therapy students. Using their existing knowledge and experience from the didactic and fieldwork portions within the curriculum, the graduate students conceived, developed, implemented, and evaluated a three-week long program. During this pilot launch of the CSLM, the course master for

Graduate Seminar established community partnerships, three months prior to implementation, at five different elementary schools. During the implementation of the program, the graduate students developed engaging handwriting and fine-motor activities for grade-level students while completing different learning objectives from the Graduate Seminar and Management & Administration courses.

At the beginning and end of the spring 2013 semester, faculty members from both courses collected data, via a 20-question student survey, as a means of exploring the accomplishment of course objectives from the student perspective. Additionally, a final reflection from students at the conclusion of the semester included seven personal reflection prompts and four program suggestion questions to be used to capture student voices to inform faculty members as to the need for course improvement.

Year Two—Spring 2014. Based on information collected from students via the survey and the reflection assignment, the implementation of CSLM continued with a new cohort of occupational therapy graduate students. At the recommendation of students from the previous cohort, the faculty members expanded the community programs component of the CSLM to include five different types of community programs serving multiple populations. To accommodate diverse student interests, four community partnerships were established that highlighted various population needs, ranging from children within after-school programs to active older adults at a senior center. In addition, students overwhelmingly desired to work with participants for a longer period of time, so each student group planned and implemented program curriculum for six weeks instead of three weeks.

Following the first year of implementation of the CSLM, a third course and an additional dimension was added. Community Practice, another course from the occupational therapy curriculum, was included (see Figure 4.3). By including this additional course, inter-cohort collaboration was facilitated with added service and leadership opportunities for other students within the program through the leaders-in-training positions.

The addition of the leaders-in-training positions allowed for enhancement of the marketing, recruiting, and personnel management components of Management & Administration, and created an element of sustainability to ensure year-to-year continuation and growth in programs and partnerships launched in Graduate Seminar. In other words, students from earlier cohorts were integrated, thereby generating a perpetual connection to the service project and community partnerships. The emphasis on communication and flexibility among faculty and students for the benefit of student learning was stressed throughout the semester to establish group members' leadership development and active collaboration. Again, at the conclusion of year two, identical survey and reflection assignments were distributed as in year one for the purpose of capturing the student voice to inform faculty members about the direction of the model and corresponding service-learning programs.

Figure 4.3. Centralized Service Learning Model: Years Two and Three

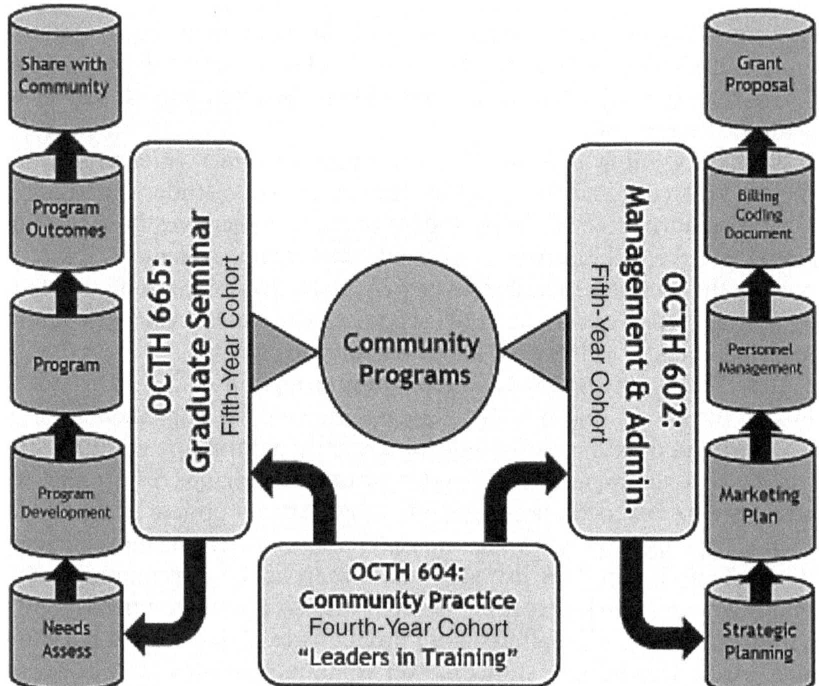

Year Three—Spring 2015. Given the established partnerships in the community, programs continued into the third year of model implementation, with the addition of new ideas from students regarding programming at current community partner locations. The students who served as leaders in training the previous year served as program managers for the spring 2015 semester. Year three programs included the same community partnerships from year two, with an additional after-school program and assisted living center for active older adults. Similar to previous years, each community group developed a unique, six-week curriculum to be implemented at respective community partnership sites. At the conclusion of year three of the CSLM, the same survey and reflection assignments were again utilized to inform faculty members about the direction of the model and corresponding service-learning programs.

Year three marked the final dimension to the CSLM. A scholarly component was added to allow a faculty member to examine the effectiveness of an actual wellness education program. More specifically, one of the launched programs, involving educating children in an after-school setting, was examined for its effectiveness and impact on the children who participated. The addition of this scholarly component to CSLM required faculty organization and preplanning. A year prior, a faculty member established a connection with a community partner to forge a partnership and to develop a preliminary timeline. This timeline included the faculty member mentoring students throughout the research process, including a research proposal for institutional review board approval.

Herein lies the critical element to collaborative teaching mentioned earlier—the ability to provide meaningful, collaborative, real-world experiences through intentional course development that includes opportunities for students and faculty, forging a shared partnership and multifaceted learning experience between the two parties. The CSLM represents the culminating cooperative and collaborative learning environment between two different courses with a central service learning experience. Based on the gradual development across three years, we believe the impact lies central to the student experience and mentorship by the faculty. To illustrate the student impact, the next section will highlight students' perceptions of the CSLM.

Student Perspectives: Centralized Service Learning Model

The CSLM, a student-driven framework, provides the foundation for the student experience that responds to a community need that students can draw from for postsecondary employability within a competitive workplace. Through the repeated application of CSLM over the course of three years, the authors have received continuous feedback based on the students' learning experiences. This section will highlight the collective feedback based on the students' point of view.

Real-World Learning Experiences and Fulfilling the Needs of a Community Partner. CSLM provides students the experience of viewing an actual community partner's perspective within the working environment, which cannot always be expressed in a textbook or classroom. Students expressed overwhelming appreciation for the opportunity to learn by doing rather than passively listening to a lecture or reading a text. Additionally, with the added benefits of creating a context for solving problems and access to an at-need population, students developed a greater understanding and social value for their directed goal and plan. The result was a sense of advocacy for the community partner as well as the clients they served. Students consistently shared the need to speak for clients who were not able to voice their needs and concerns.

Transference and Application of Developed Leadership Skills. The CSLM facilitates group leadership and interpersonal skill development. Often students indicated the need to interact and provide feedback to other team members to ensure the final product was achieved. With distributed roles within each group, some students indicated a sense of accomplishment and new-found sense of confidence leading others. Also, after initially processing the administrative-related complexities of program development and grasping how the learning objectives interconnected, the students reported freedom to focus their skill development on actual implementation of their program designs and developed leadership abilities.

Through the unique, dynamic group process embedded within the CSLM, students regularly self-monitored their group's productivity. In addition, through regular communication with the community partner, students expressed appreciation for being allowed to work autonomously and "think outside the box." This developed sense of self, willingness to take risks, and encouragement for creativity are traits employers desire (Hart Research Associates 2013).

Recommendations

Implementation of the CSLM requires attentive and systematic planning by faculty members with an inherent set of traits, one of which is being comfortable with the challenges of change. Based on the authors' repeated management of the CSLM and its multiple moving parts, success should not be determined following a one-time trial. Instead, the authors suggest a slow integration of CSLM according to the faculty member's comfort level. Given the extent of student-led work, naturally the faculty member should be comfortable taking risks, tolerant of designing assignments that build in a separate course with another faculty member of the like mindset, and most importantly, comfortable relinquishing control of the class to the students. These recommended faculty member traits also correspond to suggested actions to prepare, plan, and organize the class before the actual course launches. Additional administrative duties may be required to establish relationships within the community. For example, the faculty member should allow time to contact area organizations and should ensure internal procedures for developing formal community partnership agreements. Despite the extensive, required front-end preparation, during the semester faculty will spend much of their time mentoring and guiding students as they actively "do the work." This approach strives to encourage autonomy by developing creative, student-driven programming in the community. The faculty member serves as the conduit for constructive feedback and as a facilitator of student learning within a safe environment.

Presenting the CSLM at the beginning of the semester is an important piece of the successful implementation. The introduction must create student buy-in and provide a clear explanation of how the model will impact their learning experience. Due to the level of collaboration and integration of the service learning projects and continual embedding of multiple student learning activities, it is imperative that both of the collaborating faculty members present the CSLM as a united front. The faculty should explain the lay of the land for the semester and provide rationale for the design of the course.

Additional planning, prior to the semester, creates another opportunity to establish student leadership development. Explaining all student learning objectives is beneficial for planning purposes for student program managers. These individuals were former leaders in training and were well-versed in the program implementation the year prior. Intentionally, during the semester, faculty communicate solely with the student program managers to facilitate their leadership and allow them to take ownership of their groups; therefore, meeting with these student leaders beforehand establishes the line of communication. As a result of removing the faculty member as the perceived leader of both courses, the students naturally seek confirmation and clarification from their designated student program manager. During the pre-semester meeting with the student program managers, they are given key due dates, in effect full knowledge of all assignment expectations for both courses, which allows them to be in the know from day one. With this knowledge, student program managers can better organize the multiple moving parts of the program that often occur without direct faculty awareness. Throughout the semester, each student group works at its own pace with guidance and constructive feedback from faculty during the actual program implementation. Therefore, having student learning assignment sheets and rubrics accessible, from the start of the semester, allows student groups to transition from task to task throughout the semester with minimal faculty direction.

As exhibited by the CSLM, an opportunity exists to break down disciplinary silos within an educational program where faculty may find themselves working, all the while benefiting student learning. Application of the CSLM between professions provides faculty guidance to develop and implement interdisciplinary collaborative opportunities for students from various disciplines to engage with each other. The ever-changing world of healthcare demands faculty members create opportunities for students of varying health professions to work interprofessionally in order to prepare the graduate for entry-level work on interprofessional health teams. The World Health Organization (2010, p. 10) asserts, "Interprofessional education occurs when students from two or more professions learn about, from, and with each other to enable effective collaboration and improve health outcomes." Once students understand how to work interprofessionally, they are ready to enter the workplace as a member of the collaborative practice team. This is a key step in moving health systems from fragmentation to a position of strength. Further utilization for the CSLM includes interprofessional collaboration between healthcare students and faculty with non-health related professions, such as business, communications, and education.

The CSLM presents an innovative, collaborative-based course design framework faculty can utilize to provide meaning and engagement to students during service learning projects, while simultaneously meeting scholarly and teaching obligations. Because student engagement and active involvement are incorporated within the process, the CSLM creates a supportive structure for student–faculty collaboration with the positive end product of providing a successful and meaningful service experience. Finally, the CSLM furthers the college experience beyond the confines of campus life. Owing to the opportunity to creatively develop solutions for presented problems and analyze changing situations, the CSLM presents invaluable examples students can generalize for future productive work.

References

Barkley, Elizabeth F., Claire Howell Major, and K. Patricia Cross. 2014. *Collaborative Learning Techniques: A Handbook for College Faculty*, 2nd ed. San Francisco: John Wiley & Sons.

Blanchard, Karen. 2012. "Modeling Lifelong Learning: Collaborative Teaching Across Disciplinary Lines." *Teaching Theology & Religion* 15(4): 338–354.

Bowen, Glenn, Carol Burton, Christopher Cooper, Laura Cruz, Anna McFadden, Chesney Reich, and Melissa Warg. 2011. "Listening to the Voices of Today's Undergraduates: Implications for Teaching and Learning." *Journal of the Scholarship of Teaching & Learning* 11(3): 21–33.

Bouck, Emily C. 2007. "Co-Teaching . . . Not Just a Textbook Term: Implications for Practice." *Preventing School Failure* 51(2): 46–51.

Bruton, Dean. 2011. "Learning Creativity and Design for Innovation." *International Journal of Technology & Design Education* 21(3): 321–333.

Curseau, Petru L., and Helen Pluut. 2013. "Student Groups as Learning Entities: The Effect of Group Diversity and Teamwork Quality on Groups' Cognitive Complexity." *Studies in Higher Education* 38(1): 87–103.

Dandy, Kristina L., and Karen Bendersky. 2014. "Student and Faculty Beliefs About Learning in Higher Education: Implications for Teaching." *International Journal of Teaching and Learning in Higher Education* 26(3): 358–380.

Flinders, Brooke A. 2013. "Service-Learning Pedagogy: Benefits of a Learning Community Approach." *Journal of College Teaching & Learning* 10(3): 159–166.

Flinders, Brooke A., Matthew Dameron, and Katherine Kava. 2016. "The Development of a High-Impact Structure: Collaboration in a Service-Learning Program." In *Teaching and Learning Through Collaborative Structures*, New Directions for Teaching and Learning, edited by Jeffrey L. Bernstein and Brooke A. Flinders, 39–49. San Francisco: Jossey-Bass.

Flinders, Brooke A., Louis Nicholson, Allison Carlascio, and Katelyn Gilb. 2013. "The Partnership Model for Service-Learning Programs: A Step-By-Step Approach." *American Journal of Health Sciences* 4(2): 67–77.

Gelmon, Sherril B., Catherine Jordan, and Serena D. Seifer. 2013. "Community-Engaged Scholarship in the Academy: An Action Agenda." *Change* 45(4): 58–66.

Hart Research Associates. 2013. "It Takes More Than a Major: Employer Priorities for College Learning and Student Success." *Liberal Education* 99(2): 22–29.

Heinrich, William F., Geoffrey B. Habron, Heather L. Johnson, and Lissy Goralnik. 2015. "Critical Thinking Assessment across Four Sustainability-related Experiential Learning Settings." *Journal of Experiential Education* 38(4): 373–393.

Jacobson, Kinga. 2015. "Powerful Work-Based Learning." *Techniques: Connecting Education & Careers* 90(1): 15–19.

Johnson, Sherryl W. 2014. "Healthcare Learning Community and Student Retention." *Insight: A Journal of Scholarly Teaching* 9: 28–35.

Kalles, Susan, and Thomas G. Ryan. 2015. "Service-Learning: Promise and Possibility in Post-Secondary Education." *International Journal of Progressive Education* 11(1): 132–148.

King, Alison. 1993. "From Sage on the Stage to Guide on the Side." *College Teaching* 44(1): 30–35.
Levkoe, Charles, Shauna Brail, and Amrita Daniere. 2014. "Engaged Pedagogy and Transformative Learning in Graduate Education: A Service-Learning Case Study." *Canadian Journal of Higher Education* 44(3): 68–85.
Manor, Christopher, Stephen Bloch-Schulman, Kelly Flannery, and Peter Felten. 2010. "Foundations of Student-Faculty Partnerships in the Scholarship of Teaching and Learning." In *Engaging Student Voices in the Study of Teaching and Learning*, edited by Carmen Werder and Megan M. Otis. Sterling, VA: Stylus Publishing.
Mbugua, Tata, and Lauren Godek. 2012. "Integrating International Service-Learning in an Academic Graduate Course: An Instructor and Student Perspective." *Public Voices* 12(2): 19–37.
McDonald, James, and Lynn A. Dominguez. 2015. "Developing University and Community Partnerships: A Critical Piece of Successful Service Learning." *Journal of College Science Teaching* 44(3): 52–56.
Osterholt, Dorothy A., and Katherine Barratt. 2012. "Ideas for Practice: A Collaborative Look to the Classroom." *Journal of Developmental Education* 36(2): 22–44.
Pope-Ruark, Rebecca, Paige Ransbury, Mia Brady, and Rachel Fishman. 2014. "Student and Faculty Perspectives on Motivation to Collaborate in a Service Learning Course." *Business and Professional Communication Quarterly* 77(2): 129–149.
Rassuli, Ali, and John P. Manzer. 2005. "Teach Us to Learn: Multivariate Analysis of Perception of Success in Team Learning." *Journal of Education and Business* 81(1): 21–27.
Sabo, Samantha, Jill de Zapien, Nicolette Teufel-Shone, Cecilia Rosales, Lynda Bergsma, and Douglas Taren. 2015. "Service Learning: A Vehicle for Building Health Equity and Eliminating Health Disparities." *American Journal of Public Health* 105(S1): S38–S43.
Werder, Carmen, and Megan M. Otis, eds. 2010. *Engaging Student Voices in the Study of Teaching and Learning*. Sterling, VA: Stylus Publishing.
World Health Organization. 2010. "Framework for Action on Interprofessional Education & Collaborative Practice." *Geneva: World Health Organization*. Accessed June 2, 2015. http://whqlibdoc.who.int/hq/2010/WHO_HRH_HPN_10.3_eng.pdf
Yorio, Patrick L., and Feifei Ye. 2012. "A Meta-Analysis on the Effects of Service-Learning on the Social, Personal, and Cognitive Outcomes of Learning." *Academy of Management Learning & Education* 11(1): 9–27.

Dr. Robyn Otty is a faculty member at the Program in Occupational Therapy at Touro University Nevada in Henderson, Nevada.

Dr. Lauren Milton is a faculty member at the Program in Occupational Therapy at Washington University School of Medicine in St. Louis, Missouri.

5

Early opportunities for academic professionalization—through opportunities to teach and research in collaboration with professors—provide undergraduates with the tools needed to be successful in graduate school and in subsequent employment. Here, we advocate for more professors to consider collaboration with undergraduates, so students may practice leadership skills within the academic setting.

Exploring Academia: Professionalization and Undergraduate Collaboration

Ellen G. Galantucci, Erin Marie-Sergison Krcatovich

As recent graduates of PhD programs, we have found that collaborative learning, experienced early in one's education, can help prepare students for graduate school and their careers. Here, we will discuss our role as undergraduate collaborative learners and how that early formational opportunity has translated to crucial job preparation.

We had the unique opportunity to work closely with one of our professors, Dr. Jeffrey Bernstein at Eastern Michigan University, to serve as discussion leaders for first-year undergraduates and to meet regularly in a seminar to discuss teaching and learning. We were given a window into graduate school, and beyond, to help us better evaluate whether an advanced degree would be beneficial to us in our future employment. We have firsthand knowledge of how this early exploration of the academic world has better prepared us for the research-teaching balance of graduate school and subsequent navigation of the academic job market. Further, we benefited from these early lessons when we went on the academic job market. For example, we were better prepared to discuss *why* we teach and *how* we teach when asked by prospective employers.

The undergraduate seminar was much like a typical graduate seminar; it emphasized critical thinking, understanding academic literature, and the process of peer review. These discussions around critical concepts in learning were valuable preparation for the rigorous demands of graduate seminars. We found that we were better prepared than some of our colleagues in graduate school when asked to compose syllabi, construct course content, and begin to develop our own philosophies of teaching.

Throughout the year, the team of undergraduate discussion leaders met regularly to serve as a shared sounding board; it became a lasting network of support through graduate school and our careers afterward. We advocate for collaborative learning opportunities for undergraduates to prepare them for graduate school and future academic careers.

Problems and Strategies for Structuring an Undergraduate Collaborative Seminar

The model we propose is twofold: first, upper-level undergraduates study the scholarship of teaching and learning in a small seminar; then, the lessons are put into practice in a practical environment, such as serving as discussion leaders for first-year students. This is in keeping with classic research on teaching and learning, which has consistently shown that lecture-based classes are not the most effective for learning (Edlich 1993; McIntosh 1996; Munson 1992).

The traditional method of lecture fits the "banking model" of education, in which students believe instructors are sources of information and that they come to class each week to make "withdrawals" from the knowledge source (Freire 1970; Karp and Yoels 1976). Students are passive in the process and have little control over what or how they learn. They are not taught to think for themselves; they do not have the opportunity to consider what is important to know and to understand. This method has been described as "contrary to almost every principle of optimal settings for student learning" (Guskin 1994, p. 17).

In contrast, the "Learning Paradigm" calls for an increased focus on student learning, which includes allowing students a more active role in their own education. To achieve optimal learning, students should be more collaborative with their instructors (Barr and Tagg 1995). In this format, students and instructors "co-learn" by having a dialogue rather than a monologue (Wright 1985).

To effectively co-learn, as in the learning-paradigm model, undergraduate teaching assistants work directly with the instructor to help achieve classroom goals. This relationship has been found to improve learning among the students in the classroom. In addition, research has shown that this method has encouraged growth among the undergraduate teaching assistants by encouraging them to be more active learners (Adler 1993; Hensley and Oakley 1998). It helped these assistants to recognize the different learning styles among students, to understand the material much better than they had when they initially took the course, and to feel more confident when speaking in public (Fingerson and Culley 2001).

Another strategy for moving away from the lecture-based classroom is a seminar format that involves a discussion between instructors and students. This format encourages students to develop critical-thinking skills (Garside 1996) and retain information (Steffens 1989) better than in lecture classes. Students are more likely to ask questions when they do not understand (Crone 2001), which better prepares them for life after college. This method is generally used in graduate schools, because the expectation is that students are beginning to produce their own knowledge and work rather than simply repeating the knowledge from their instructor (Sullivan 1991).

In our experience, even advanced undergraduate students generally have limited exposure to these alternative methods of learning. Would using these methods in combination help to equip students with the tools to help them succeed in graduate school and careers as academics? Particularly for students intending to continue their education beyond a bachelor's degree, there may be few opportunities to learn beyond the lecture format, which can leave them ill-prepared for their future.

Our Experiences as Undergraduate Collaborators

As undergraduates, we were unsure of what to expect in graduate school before deciding to pursue an advanced degree ourselves. What will we be expected to research, to read, to experience? What happens in a small graduate seminar, and how is that different from undergraduate courses? What is involved in the threefold life of academics—research, teaching, and service? Professors who wish to better prepare their students for graduate school and postgraduate careers can structure undergraduate seminars, such as the one we will describe, that mimic the small course size and demanding study of these programs.

Simulation and Seminar Design. In 2005–2006, we facilitated in-class congressional simulations for an American Government course, mostly comprised of first-year students. For three to four weeks of the semester, the students in the course, modeling a legislature, would write bills and discuss them with their classmates in the hope of passing new laws related to a particular political topic, such as affirmative action and the War on Terror. The students also wrote pre-simulation papers, which outlined their initial thoughts on the topic for the week, and post-simulation papers, which reflected on their experiences working with their classmates. As upper-class political science majors, our responsibilities included leading discussion during the simulation rounds, providing probing questions and prompts to encourage them to think more "deeply," and selecting reading material to discuss. We also read the reflection papers to help us understand what students thought prior to the simulation and how they interpreted the events after they had occurred. We did not grade student papers; we did, however, offer input to the professor on participation grades for the students in the simulation.

In addition to facilitating the simulations, we participated in an advanced seminar on the scholarship of teaching and learning (SoTL). The facilitators met separately each week to collaborate on our progress throughout the semester and study the scholarship on how college students learn. We discussed how to prepare for simulations and our reactions to them after they occurred. We also discussed the students' papers that we read, because this was the first time most of us had really thought about how other students write or about the grading process. The seminar provided crucial peer-to-peer intellectual and emotional support during the initial process of our "learning" how to teach.

Undergraduate Collaborative Project Design. Undergraduate collaborative learning opportunities like ours can be structured to fit any classroom and discipline. Based on our experience, we recommend that some basic characteristics be incorporated, as specified in the following four subsections:

Small Sized Seminar, Which Meets Regularly. In any collaborative learning environment, the smaller-sized seminar will allow each student to know the others well, promote trust, and develop community. We recommend that the class size stay under 10 students, whenever possible, and that it meet at least biweekly throughout the course of a semester or, if possible, academic year.

Opportunity to Collaborate on a Larger Project. This project can be a large laboratory experiment, community service, helping assemble materials for a study guide in an introductory course, a public presentation of research findings, or anything that is appropriate for the discipline.

Provocative Readings for Discussion. Unlike most undergraduate courses, our collaborative learning environment had no textbook. Rather, we were immersed in the professional literature of the discipline, including material on teaching in political science, developing civic engagement, and addressing the needs of adult students as learners. This can be tailored to any project; students will benefit from the opportunity to challenge themselves with more difficult readings and discussions than they would find in the average classroom. Furthermore, if they can participate in the process of choosing readings throughout the seminar, they will benefit all the more from time spent considering what to share with their peers. Students are used to being told which material is important; this gives them a rare opportunity to consider the importance of material themselves.

Flexibility, with Defined Goals. Although we advocate for the students to be active participants in the process, the professor should serve as a guide to help students anticipate areas of difficulty and work through them. The key is to select a project with many opportunities for students to participate in the creation of new material and to discuss the challenges that can arise. Collaboration, by its nature, requires that the students are not carrying out the professor's game plan but, rather, sharing some degree of responsibility for the final outcome.

Academic and Professional Benefits. Our weekly discussion-leader meetings proved to be invaluable for our professional preparation for PhD programs after graduation. We began learning the language of academic dialogue and became comfortable with the idea that colleagues debate and sometimes disagree over scholarship. This helped prepare us for graduate school's rigorous seminars. The structure of graduate school felt more natural after experiencing the small classroom size of our weekly leadership meetings.

In our experience, graduate school is much more collaborative in nature than undergraduate studies. The biggest change in style was the expectation of active seminar participation in graduate school that did not exist in most of our undergraduate classes. In particular, the answers to the questions changed. In most undergraduate classes, instructors asked questions that were either opinion-based or for which there was a right or wrong answer. In graduate school, the answers were analysis-based. When discussing theories of political science in graduate classes, we created theories of our own. This mirrored our experiences in our undergraduate seminars in which we analyzed theories of teaching. Our goals were not to answer a question correctly on an exam or to find the answer that our professors expected us to produce, but to collaborate to solve real-world problems with the best explanations possible. In our discussion-leader positions, rather than individually competing for grades, we worked together to define and address issues that affected the American Government students in the simulations; this proved to be good practice for the collaborative style of learning we later found in graduate school.

Professionally, we also felt more confident engaging our colleagues in conversations about the scholarship of teaching and learning as we moved from undergraduate studies into, and beyond, graduate programs ourselves. We felt comfortable seeking other sources of teaching support during graduate school, within and outside our academic discipline. This helped us to bring attention in our respective departments to the creative and important work in the scholarship of teaching and learning. This dialogue encouraged our colleagues to improve their own teaching as they considered their classroom techniques, sometimes for the first time.

Although many of our colleagues avoided teaching, we felt encouraged and supported to begin teaching our own courses as soon as possible. We were both teaching by the summer after our third year of graduate studies. With the experiences as undergraduates behind us, we had a foundation from which to begin. Most importantly, in those first weeks as new teachers, we knew that we would make mistakes and continue to learn about teaching with each new class. We were eager to begin. Ellen taught earlier than most of her cohort, for more classes per week, and sought her first teaching experience outside her university after just four years, first as an adjunct, then as a full-time lecturer. Erin designed online and in-person classes, beginning with facilitating a discussion section and following that with opportunities to design and teach for very large (100+ students) and very small (fewer than 10) classes, both within and outside her university, before graduation. We can honestly say that the opportunities to give so much thought to teaching prior to our first classes were invaluable in preparing us—perhaps much more so than many of our colleagues.

Lessons from the Undergraduate Collaborative Seminar

With our experiences as discussion leaders in mind, we would like to highlight several lessons learned in these early professionalization experiences that we believe to be highly beneficial and transferable across many classrooms and disciplines. In the seminar, we emphasized the creation of a learner-centered environment that was able to meet changing needs, and that was feedback-driven and collegial. When we began to design our own classes, these lessons proved invaluable.

First, our undergraduate seminar was learner-centered. The focus was primarily on *how* our students in the simulation would learn. We discussed various learning styles, the impact of quality materials for the classroom, and the difficulties of reaching all students, all the time. Each week, our seminar would consider various theories of research, which prepared us for both the simulation classroom and, later, for exposure to various streams of research in graduate school. We have applied these lessons to our own classrooms. Since our first teaching experiences in graduate school, our students have reacted much more positively to a learner-centered environment, and our experience as educators has been much more enjoyable, when we focused more on *how* students learned, rather than on *what* was learned. Our students have reported higher levels of satisfaction than many of our graduate student instructor and faculty peers, on average.

Second, our seminar as undergraduates was not fully formed on the first day of the semester. Rather, we were encouraged to bring in articles or chapters to share with each other, and were allowed to develop the discussion organically around issues that we experienced facilitating the simulations. We can appreciate how different this teaching model was from many of our courses as undergraduates and, as a result, it had a profound impact on our own teaching philosophies. We both have found that flexibility is the key to course design, particularly knowing when to adapt the course "midstream" to meet the intellectual demands of the class. This is a very scary thing to do — it is difficult to let go of the reins a bit and allow the class to change when needed.

Third, our own feedback in the simulation and seminar helped develop future iterations of the same seminar for others. Although we were in the first seminar group, it blossomed into a program offered regularly, which benefited many other undergraduates over time. We believe in allowing new material and content to develop out of student feedback; this student-driven model is one that we have had the joys of experiencing as students and now implement in our own classes.

Finally, we actively worked to create a positive classroom culture of collegiality and support. Each week, our undergraduate seminar cohort built up one another as we shared our high and low moments in the classroom. Thus, we came to understand that there is not a perfect way to teach; rather, there are many approaches and mistakes can and will happen. This helped ease some of the fears of teaching on our own and changed the direction of our professional careers for the better. When we began teaching, we felt comfortable trying new things in the classroom, even with the risk of making mistakes, because we knew we could recover from them and because we believed our students would learn more due to our attention to improving their classroom experience.

Professional Impact

Undergraduate collaboration is perhaps more common in other disciplines, such as the hard sciences, than it is in the social sciences. We encourage other departments to offer ways for upper-level students to team-teach or co-facilitate. As discussed earlier, these opportunities have had a tremendous impact on our professional careers. Since neither of us studied education as undergraduates, the exposure to academia encouraged us to seek careers in higher education and further helped to prepare us for teaching our own courses. In particular, our experiences impacted course development, course management, and our ability to discuss and analyze our courses.

Course Development. When participating in the collaborative seminar, we realized that students care about very diverse issues and will be most successful when they are invested in the course. From our first experience as simulation facilitators, we had the opportunity to read students' papers and began to understand that there is an art to creating assignments that give students ample room to thrive. Wanting to build up learner-centered classrooms, we now structure our courses to include ways for students to pursue their own interests. We have both crafted writing assignments where students were asked, for example, to critique a specific federal policy of their choosing. Many students discuss issues in their own areas of study, such as education majors writing about No Child Left Behind or criminal justice majors considering the use of the death penalty. This choice gives the students an opportunity to direct their own learning in a way that is beneficial to them personally and professionally.

Having had the experience of developing our own course materials, it was easier as graduate assistants to develop our first syllabi. In particular, we felt equipped to explain our choices of reading material and assignments to the students, giving them the rationale behind our course design. Our students appreciated this attention to their learning. In some introductory classes, students do not read the textbook and say that it is too dry or irrelevant. We have learned to mitigate this by bringing in outside readings for such classes so students can better see how to apply the material. In consideration of the use of such content, students have written comments such as

"I also enjoyed the out-of-class online assignments. They were always very interesting and it was cool to see how well they correlated with the chapter from that week."

Course Management. Since we were able to flexibly adapt our own learning material as the semester progressed, we learned that faculty members can, and often do, incorporate new material, examples, and current events "on the fly" as the semester progresses, depending on the students' needs and interests. This helped us get over an initial, and ultimately incorrect, instinct to control our class with a rigidly set lesson plan and lecture, to the detriment of students' learning.

These changes to courses have occurred in some way in nearly every course we have taught. At times, this flexibility has meant including extra readings that were added during the course of the semester. For example, when the Supreme Court heard *United States v. Windsor* (2013), Ellen discussed the U.S. court system in her American Government class and brought in additional material to help the class understand and respond to the case. The students were more enthusiastic than students in many other semesters, because the case was relevant and ongoing, on a topic that mattered to them. Flexibility can include going so far as adding extra days to the semester, listed as "to be decided" on the syllabus, to allow students time to discuss a topic of their choosing, work on research papers, or correct homework errors. This has allowed the personality of the class to dictate the best direction for the class. The flexibility allows students to have more of an influence over the course than exists in most classes.

Most importantly perhaps is the confidence to design different classes in very different ways. We have seen positive results from courses developed out of student feedback. Just like students do not all learn the same way, material can be taught in many different ways; a one-size-fits-all approach to course design is inefficient and ineffective for learning. Although many instructors find a style that works in one class and apply it to all others, the experience of contemplating course design in a seminar setting helped us to consider each class individually, without feeling we were tied to one style.

Course Analysis and Dialogue. Our confidence as instructors grew over the course of the year spent as undergraduate facilitators. We developed a new vocabulary to discuss teaching and began developing informed opinions on what constitutes quality instruction. This has formed the backbone of our interest in teaching throughout graduate school and beyond. As PhD candidates, we pursued opportunities to work with other graduate students to study teaching at the college level, within and outside of our discipline. We have felt better equipped on the job market to discuss teaching strategies and philosophies in concrete terms, including offering specific examples of how we have put our teaching philosophies into practice in the classroom. Ultimately, this has given us a competitive advantage on the job market, as many hiring universities want to know about their instructors' experiences with and perspectives on teaching at the college level.

One of the most common questions we have received on the job market is how we would promote civic engagement if hired. Universities want students to have opportunities to work with their communities and learn outside the classroom. This is the essence of a classroom culture of collegiality and support. Because we have thought about our role as instructors since long before we were instructors ourselves, we have many ideas about how to help students to get more out of their college experience. We recognize that so much student learning occurs outside the textbook, and we focus on developing ideas about what helps students most in their future careers. The ability to discuss this in depth has helped us to set ourselves apart from other job candidates.

Closing Remarks

Increased confidence, greater satisfaction with our education, and preparation for our future careers are but a few of the ways that structured undergraduate collaboration has helped us to develop as professionals. In closing, we wish to emphasize that our experiences were both unique and universal. The general structure of the collaborative seminar is one that we feel would benefit many disciplines. We have found that the opportunity to work closely with a professor in our field, experiencing both the rigors of graduate-school seminars and the demands and joys of teaching, has been tremendously important in our own academic careers. We entered graduate school more prepared and far more confident than many of our peers to teach our own students. We have carried these lessons beyond graduate school to our own professional lives. Whether it is a simulation, laboratory supervision, leading a reading group, or any other appropriate opportunity for undergraduates to mentor or "peer teach" other students, a collaborative design can only strengthen the learning opportunity.

In keeping with the idea of student voices in the scholarship of teaching and learning, this collaborative work offers opportunities to focus on dialogue with students and instructors. We strongly believe that co-learning—working together on the course topics—is the key to preparation for academic life. For students who are seeking other careers, these are necessary skills in all professional endeavors. In all types of jobs, individuals must learn to respectfully disagree, to defend their positions on projects, to occasionally serve as peer mentors to other, perhaps newer, employees, and to work together amicably to achieve group goals. We encourage other instructors to consider ways in which their own undergraduate students would benefit from working directly with them to design, facilitate, and discuss classes at their university.

Disclaimer

The views expressed in this chapter are those of the authors and do not reflect official views or policies of the U.S. Bureau of Labor Statistics.

References

Adler, Patricia A. 1993. "Personalizing Mass Education: The Assistant Teaching Assistant (ATA) Program." *Teaching Sociology* 21(2): 172–176.

Barr, Robert B., and John Tagg. 1995. "From Teaching to Learning: A New Paradigm for Undergraduate Education." *Change* 27(6): 13–25.

Crone, James A. 2001. "Attaining More and Greater Depth of Discussing in the Undergraduate Classroom: The Seminar and Seminar Paper." *Teaching Sociology* 29(2): 229–236.

Edlich, Richard F. 1993. "My Last Lecture." *Journal of Emergency Medicine* 11(6): 771–774.

Fingerson, Laura, and Aaron B. Culley. 2001. "Collaborators in Teaching and Learning: Undergraduate Teaching Assistants in the Classroom." *Teaching Sociology* 29(6): 299–315.

Freire, Paulo. 1970. *Pedagogy of the Oppressed*. New York: Seabury.

Garside, Colleen. 1996. "Look Who's Talking: A Comparison of Lecture and Group Discussion Teaching Strategies in Developing Critical Thinking Skills." *Communication Education* 45(3): 212–227.

Guskin, Alan E. 1994. "Reducing Costs and Enhancing Student Learning." *Change* 26(4): 16–25.

Hensley, Thomas R., and Maureen Oakley. 1998. "The Challenge of the Large Lecture Class: Making It More Like a Small Seminar." *PS: Political Science and Politics* 31(1): 47–51.

Karp, David A., and William C. Yoels. 1976. "The College Classroom: Some Observations on the Meanings of Student Participation." *Sociology and Social Research* 60(4): 421–439.

McIntosh, Noel. 1996. *Why Do We Lecture? JHPIEGO Strategy Paper #2*. Baltimore: JHPIEGO.

Munson, Lawrence S. 1992. *How to Conduct Training Seminars: A Complete Reference Guide for Training Managers and Professionals*. New York: McGraw-Hill.

Steffens, Henry. 1989. "Collaborative Learning in a History Seminar." *The History Teacher* 22(2): 125–138.

Sullivan, Theresa A. 1991. "Making the Graduate Curriculum Explicit." *Teaching Sociology* 19(3): 408–413.

Wright, Richard A. 1985. "Curing 'Doonesbury's Disease': A Prescription for Dialogue in the Classroom." *Quarterly Journal of Ideology* 9(4): 3–8.

ELLEN G. GALANTUCCI is a statistician at the U.S. Bureau of Labor Statistics. She has a Bachelors degree from Eastern Michigan University and a PhD from the University of North Carolina in political science. She has previously taught at UNC, North Carolina State University, and High Point University.

ERIN MARIE-SERGISON KRCATOVICH has a BA from Eastern Michigan University and a PhD in political science from Michigan State University. She is a lecturer at San Jacinto College in Houston, teaching political science. Her primary research is concerned with nonprofit behavior and public policy.

6

Four different perspectives—from the director of a scholarship of teaching and learning dialogue forum, the director of a leadership institute, and two undergraduate students—join together to discuss a collaboration in optimizing leadership education at Western Washington University.

Collaborating in Dialogue for an Optimal Leadership Education

Carmen Werder, Joseph Garcia, Jamie Bush, Caroline Dallstream

Leadership development is a topic of great current interest with books on leadership abounding as society confronts many challenges and, some would even say, when we may be experiencing a crisis of leadership in our national legislative bodies. Recent book titles featured on Amazon range from provocative ones like *Leaders Eat Last* (Sinek 2014) to straightforward titles like *Leadership Skills: How to be an Influential, Respectful, and Successful Leader* (Good 2015). Yet while leadership books, workshops, courses, and camps abound, and leadership activities routinely appear on school programs, leadership is a subject that higher education institutions rarely require alongside English, mathematics, science, and the arts, or even in its home disciplines in the social sciences. As a result, leadership represents a domain that seems familiar to everyone, but without any widely accepted curriculum—or shared pedagogy—to guide our teaching and learning. As co-authors, we have come to realize that students can learn leadership lessons and practice leadership skills whether or not an institution calls them by name. In this chapter, we attempt to illustrate a collaborative approach to building a leadership education.

This approach pairs a formal, research-based curricular structure, which provides a language for capturing leadership lessons, with a co-curricular structure that enables students to enact the phenomenon of leadership in the context of a dialogue on teaching and learning.

Leadership Education over Time: Joseph Garcia's Reflections

I have had the privilege of being a student of leadership and the founding director of the Karen W. Morse Institute of Leadership at Western Washington

University. In my tenure as director of the institute, I had the opportunity to apply my understandings of leadership across the campus. My experience collaborating with our Teaching-Learning Academy (TLA), and the students who participated in the work of the institute, is most relevant here. These students taught me that leadership development is nonlinear and particularistic, even though leadership processes are relatively predictable and common. Furthermore, our approach to leadership learning attempted to balance structure and spontaneity by emphasizing the importance of building effective relationships. By this balance, I mean developing relationships with the TLA director and staff, the executives who participated in our program, faculty from across campus who nominated students to participate in institute activities, and the students and staff who offered leadership opportunities in student clubs.

Leadership education, as an evolving field, reflects how the definition of leadership itself has changed over time. Leadership development in the United States initially focused on nurturing an individual's character such that certain leadership qualities (e.g., assertiveness, extraversion, and ability to command authority) were imbued in the prospective leader. As a result, the focal point of these instructive efforts was on the individual. This approach was consistent with the nineteenth-century notion of the "Great Man" leadership prototype (Carlyle 1907), which emphasized the qualities of an individual who functioned as a leader. This focus on the individual was influential in leadership research and education into the mid-twentieth century (Stogdill 1948). In contrast, and riding the intellectual popularity of behaviorism, developing behaviors, such as being directive and considerate, became the focus of leadership education by the mid-twentieth century. As leadership researchers embraced this behavioral view, the concept of leadership shifted from a focus on the individual to a focus on a set of identifiable behaviors that individuals could become proficient at performing as required by various situations (Fleishman 1953; Hersey and Blanchard 1969).

More recently, leadership scholars have reconceptualized leadership as a relationship-based, situated phenomenon which acknowledges the quality of the interaction between participants in a particular context. A representative current definition of leadership includes the following elements (Nahavandi 2015, p. 3):

- Leadership is a group and social phenomenon.
- Leadership involves interpersonal influence.
- Leadership is action- and goal-directed.
- Leadership involves some form of hierarchy within a group.

This perspective significantly broadens the conceptualization of leadership and, in the process, recognizes more people than the formal leader as the focus of leadership. As a consequence, leadership educators face new and significant challenges in addressing this more nuanced and complex nature of leadership. Put simply, the traditional top down, authority-driven leadership view of the past is no longer adequate as a model for explaining leadership development.

A New Leadership Model and the Need for Collaboration

The old leadership model, embodied in past leadership definitions and typified in stable and large institutions, reflected a social order that was reliable and predictable wherein institutions, such as governments and universities as well as their central administrators, exerted powerful influence over the lives of most people in their purviews. Today's world is quite different. We fight wars differently, we structure companies differently, and our social relationships are far more dynamic and fluid in nature. Perhaps the most significant shift in the twenty-first century is the way that the Internet and social media have prompted a decentralization of information access, a shift that has challenged traditional institutions and led to a new relational and collaborative approach to leadership and organizations (Mele 2013). We now have networked organizations and structures that are project-based with participants who have an allegiance to a task or cause, but not necessarily to an organization or institution. Leadership in this environment requires an approach that is more personally engaging and less defined by formal roles and responsibilities than in the past. In this context, successful leadership development requires working across collaborative structures.

Our Story

At Western Washington University, we were fortunate to establish in 2010 the Karen W. Morse Institute for Leadership Studies, tasked with developing academically credible, interdisciplinary curricular programs in leadership (www.wwu.edu/leadership/morse/). The institute was conceived with the expectation that it would partner with initiatives across campus, some of which were explicitly identified in terms of leadership such as Western's Leadership Advantage (www.wwu.edu/leadership/) and others that provided leadership learning opportunities, but were not formally recognized as leadership education sites such as the Teaching-Learning Academy (http://library.wwu.edu/tla_objectives).

The core functions of the institute included developing academic courses in leadership studies that would complement programs that provided experiential education and job/internship placements with a leadership focus. To this end, the institute launched a targeted program for entering first-year students expressing an interest in leadership. It also created its first leadership cohort, whose members began with a foundational course in leadership studies and who could then pursue studies in any area and were encouraged to participate in co-curricular programs in more formal leadership capacities. Finally, the institute offered a large section, Introduction to Leadership Studies class satisfying a social science general education requirement and attracting first- and second-year students with wide-ranging academic interests. The course is set up to include both a large lecture format focused on leadership theory and research accompanied by small group discussion sessions emphasizing learning about being leaders (i.e., self-assessments and reflections) and practicing leadership (i.e., leadership simulations and experiential exercises; see Snook 2008). The lecture section meets twice a week, and the small group discussion sessions, led by two advanced leadership students who facilitate conversations and activities, meet once a week in a two-hour format.

As noted earlier, the more senior leadership students facilitate the discussion sections and concurrently take a 400-level seminar in leadership pedagogy. Recruitment for these students occurs through a nomination process by faculty and staff from across the campus with the objective of enhancing students' leadership potential as they develop in their chosen field of study or professional interest. The students are diverse in terms of race, gender, academic, and professional interests. They are special in that they have already established themselves as engaged and successful students in the eyes of faculty, staff, and peers.

The advanced course provides them support for leading learning in the introductory leadership study discussion sessions and assists them in being responsible for managing their weekly sessions for the full 10 weeks of the academic term. They also engage in group discussions with several senior-level executives from the business, educational, nonprofit, and government sectors to discuss leadership development and the challenges in helping people achieve group goals. As their capstone project, they create an individual leadership development plan, in which they assess their own strengths and shortcomings and map them onto the opportunities and challenges they envision for their futures in an array of leadership environments.

These courses are now in their fifth year and have spawned a minor in leadership studies. Furthermore, students who have completed the introductory course are better informed on how to be nominated and selected for the advanced course by virtue of observing their near-peers as facilitators in the course and learning about the opportunities that exist in the university for developing their leadership potential. Perhaps most important is the enactment of the core principles of leadership by developing relationships between the institute and co-curricular programs, staff development programs, participating academic departments across campus, and external participants such as senior executives in the community. As an organization, the institute works to embody the form of leadership that it teaches. These alliances reinforce in word and deed the overarching belief that leadership is about building and enhancing relationships, as leaders, as followers, and as stakeholders in the community.

In the next section, we offer the learning experiences from two students who completed the advanced leadership studies course and who also participated and contributed as leaders in the TLA.

Learning to Lead through Dialogue: Caroline Dallstream's Reflections

Before coming to college, I didn't think about leadership as part of my academics. I experienced the idea of it in extracurricular activities such as sports and clubs and even in my social life, but it wasn't a subject I thought about learning in the classroom. As a senior at Western, I now experience leadership in an entirely new light. This attitude changed in my first year at WWU when I started to work for the TLA. TLA is a dialogue-based forum where participants explore questions about the teaching and learning environment at Western and then actively work to improve that environment based on their conclusions. Meetings are structured to facilitate dialogue with a focus on equitable exploration of ideas from students, faculty, staff, and community member participants within a flattened hierarchy. It was my work with TLA—in which student staff members help facilitate small dialogue groups, respectfully and productively work with others to maintain group goals, and encourage multiple perspectives—that resulted in the TLA director nominating me for the Leadership Studies 450 course. In the discussion section of this leadership course, we learned leadership theory, which gave me the language and concepts necessary to name and analyze my previous leadership experiences. It also provided a structure for reflection and for an exploration of different styles and methods of leadership. The other half of this course included co-leading a discussion section of an associated Leadership Studies 101 course.

As I learned and practiced the connection between the dialogue that was so central to TLA and the concepts and practices from the leadership course, my own personal leadership style emerged. I began to see myself as an effective facilitator of ideas. I saw the profound influence dialogue could have on individuals and on groups. For individuals, dialogue can be empowering. By creating a space for the respectful exploration of ideas, individuals receive the opportunity to voice their ideas, and, for many students, it may be the first time they have expressed ideas candidly about themselves as learners, about their fears, about their dreams. That very voicing can increase their confidence and clarify their thoughts. Individuals can feel valued and can grow through the exploration of diverse perspectives. Empowered individuals become leaders through the dialogue itself. I know that I did.

The collective group benefits from dialogue as well. The structure of dialogue invites creativity and thoroughness simultaneously and results in richer and better decision making. Also, dialogue over time (even for just a 10-week term) fosters the development of trusting relationships that allow individuals to know each other so that a group can divide tasks according to an individual's strengths. Most importantly, the connections that form from dialogue are strong and create resilient and supportive groups of people who care about each other and about the projects they are working on together. For these reasons, I strive to create spaces for dialogue whenever I can, whether I'm the designated leader or not.

My leadership education has made me a leader of idea-making. I have learned and practiced guiding dialogue by prompting questions, summarizing ideas, and finding connections across perspectives, thereby facilitating the discovery of shared meaning. These practices can contribute to good dialogue and have influenced how I perceive a creative and resilient team, as well as my personal role. I would not have learned as much about myself or about group dynamics if I had only studied learning theory. Simply put, I learned to lead through dialogue. The foundation I received in my leadership studies and in TLA even led me to successfully apply for a study abroad program for a quarter in Patagonia with the National Outdoor Leadership School, which enhanced my understanding of leadership further. Now I'm headed for a career that combines my love of the outdoors with my regard for leadership studies.

We offer Caroline's story to point to a lesson learned: A leader emerges in dialogue with others in the process of meaning-making. To lead wisely and well requires a keen sense of judgment that cannot grow in isolation, but rather relies on the continuous interplay between an individual's evolving views in the context of others. A leader knows how to facilitate the discovery of shared meaning. However, as Jamie Bush's story will suggest next, that facilitation might happen backward by design.

Learning to Lead from Behind: Jamie Bush's Reflections

On the brink of graduation from Western Washington University, I have had many opportunities to take on leadership positions. As a student member of the TLA staff for three years, like Caroline, I also learned early on how to facilitate small-group dialogue sessions. In contrast with the discussion groups I later facilitated for lower division students in the leadership studies course, my role in these TLA dialogue sessions has been to assist faculty, staff, and student participants from across campus, as well as community members, to deepen our collective understanding of particular teaching- and learning-related topics.

In addition to engaging a mixed group of participants rather than just students, the TLA conversational model also contrasts with the typical classroom model of conversation in that it relies on a distinction between *discussion* and *dialogue*. Elinor and Gerard (1998) define *dialogue* in terms of its primary goal: to discover shared meaning. In contrast, they define *discussion* in terms of its primary aim: to identify the optimal answer or solution in a particular situation. This fundamental distinction accounts for how TLA works. Responding to a shared BIG question that we collectively determine every fall term, TLA *dialogue* groups work to use our own lived experiences in the academy to address each year's BIG question. Although it was part of my work study position to both facilitate and scribe these dialogue groups, I never thought of myself as particularly skilled at doing it—until after I served as a mentor in the leadership-studies course.

As a result of my experiences in both the upper-level leadership course and in facilitating and scribing TLA sessions, I have come to understand an important lesson: A leadership education should allow students to explore what being a leader entails in multiple contexts and to expand our sense of our own leadership skills. I have come to believe that leadership exhibits itself in different ways. All students will likely show leadership skills in their educational careers at least once; knowing the skills of a successful leader will permit students and others to recognize that leadership potential. Because of my nomination for the leadership course and through serving as a mentor for first-year students, I learned that there are leadership opportunities even for introverts. I gained the ability to lead from behind. The term *leading from behind* acknowledges a whole set of skills that can enable leadership actions. A leader can lead quietly, but effectively. In taking the advanced leadership class, I was able to both recognize and name this ability in myself while guiding the Introduction to Leadership Studies students in recognizing it in themselves. Despite being an introvert, I learned that I could facilitate activities that enabled the lower division students to envision and simulate the actions leaders might exhibit in various situations. In short, I led them from behind, from my position as a student mentor.

This experience also complemented and enhanced my role as a student staff member of the TLA. Facilitating small-group dialogues is a huge part of my responsibility in the TLA; by also facilitating student discussion groups in the leadership studies course, I came to see myself as a listening, facilitative leader. In the process, I gained a greater sense of agency in facilitating mixed groups that crossed power differentials not only at the university but also with participants from outside the university. After taking the leadership course, I noticed that, while facilitating these small TLA dialogues, I was able to listen more than talk. I would ask prompting questions that allowed the participants in my group to take a leadership role themselves. I learned to create an environment that is safe and open, an ability that I now understand as crucial in leadership development.

In fact, I have discovered that being an introvert may even be particularly useful in creating such an open, listening environment. In an older model of leadership, my introversion may have caused me to be overlooked, but my TLA supervisor recognized in me some kind of desire to assume a more engaged role and, apparently, some skill I was not even aware of. As a peer leadership mentor, I watched other students taking note of my quiet approach and observed many of them start to speak and question more. I learned that the most crucial part of being able to lead is the capacity to create a safe and open environment where risk taking is allowed. Such a space provides a sanctuary for people to feel encouraged to take on responsibility, even if they don't succeed at first. The TLA format, which we call structured informality, cultivates this kind of risk-taking community by flattening the usual institutional hierarchy that would set up a conception that only the people in charge can be in leadership positions. In fact, the students who facilitate the dialogue groups have more agency in influencing the dialogue than the faculty, staff, and community participants.

By serving in these facilitative roles both in the leadership studies class and in TLA, I learned that I have long had the latent skill to lead from behind. Now that I have focused energy on deliberately cultivating it, others now look to me to provide leadership. Coming to this realization has allowed me to see that my introversion is not a weakness, and I feel proud of the influence I can have on others, simply by being interested in their ideas. Understanding the value of being able to lead from behind and actually doing it has helped in the formation of my identity. I gained the knowledge that everyone can lead, and by showing, rather than only telling, I am helping develop leaders who can do the same for others.

We offer Jamie's story as an illustration of a second lesson learned: Leaders need to be skilled communicators, not just in how they speak but perhaps even more critically in how they listen, if they are going to facilitate the discovery of deeper, shared understandings as well help facilitate problem-solving in the company of others.

Recognizing Collaborative Leaders: Carmen Werder's Reflections

As director of our Teaching-Learning Academy, I have had the good fortune of learning about leadership both from the director of our leadership institute and from student leaders like my colleagues here. From Joe, I have learned the importance of seeking out potential student leaders who may not match the typical profile. By soliciting nominations for the leadership studies mentoring course from across the university, he sent a clear message: Leaders are everywhere. They just need to be called out. Instead of simply turning to the usual suspects in sites such as student government, he helped many of us see students we were already working with in a new way. His invitation also served as an impetus for me to recognize emergent leaders and to respond to my own programmatic needs. The TLA needs students who can facilitate relationships, not simply perform well on individual tasks. In recommending Caroline and Jamie, for example, I was addressing a staffing need. Not only did they take advantage of the leadership-mentoring course and gain personal leadership skills, they came away as better TLA facilitators as a result of their participation in the course. They made TLA better, perhaps mainly because they gained a new appreciation for their own agency in leading others. And I learned that part of my role as a designated leader is to identify students who are on their way to becoming leaders and provide structured opportunities to advance their development.

From students like Caroline and Jamie, I have also learned a huge lesson about what it means to be a collaborative leader. As Chrislip (2002) emphasizes, effective collaborative leaders are not domineering. Rather, they know "how to encourage and support the participation of others ... how to acknowledge and celebrate the successes of others without taking credit ... how to lead as peers rather than as superiors" (p. 14). Watching these two quiet, unassuming students become such effective leaders has helped me temper my own tendencies to lead too forcefully. Learning to lead, like learning to collaborate, requires a fundamental humility and openness to being led.

Discovering Leadership Learning Communities

Together, we have learned a crucial lesson: To receive an optimal leadership education, we all need ongoing opportunities—both formal and informal—to learn and lead *in* dialogue with others. Leadership development is a life-long journey best done in the company of others who share an interest in making the same journey. We cannot assume that once a keen sense of self as a leader emerges it will persist for any of us in some kind of permanent static state, and in a vacuum, unless we have ongoing venues for responsible leadership in multiple contexts. Because of its basis in relational learning, leadership needs to be continually fostered in community with others. Taken together, our stories have also helped us to understand that an optimal leadership education results from deliberately co-designing interrelationships between curricular and co-curricular experiences and structures. As Bass (2012) suggests in acknowledging how we have "disrupted ourselves" in higher education by neglecting the high impact practices often found in co-curricular sites, we need to "design for great fluidity and connection between formal curriculum and the experiential co-curriculum" (p. 5). On an institutional level, how might we more intentionally recognize existing structures that seem to have an affinity for each other and for our shared leadership work? We have much to gain, not only by developing individual leaders, but also by developing informed leadership communities that lead together and collaborative structures that enable and liberate those partnerships.

References

Bass, Randy. 2012. "Disrupting Ourselves: The Problem of Learning in Higher Education." *EDUCAUSE Review* 47(2): 1–14.

Carlyle, Thomas. 1907. *Heroes and Hero Worship*. Boston: Adams.

Chrislip, David D. 2002. *The Collaborative Leadership Fieldbook*. San Francisco: Jossey-Bass.

Elinor, Linda, and Glenna Gerard. 1998. *Dialogue: Rediscover the Transforming Power of Conversation*. Hoboken, NJ: John Wiley & Sons.

Fleishman, Edwin A. 1953. "The Measurement of Leadership Attitudes in Industry." *Journal of Applied Psychology* 37(3): 153–158.

Good, Henry. 2015. *Leadership Skills: How to Be an Influential, Respectful, and Successful Leader*. Amazon Digital Services.

Hersey, Paul, and Kenneth H. Blanchard. 1969. "Life Cycle Theory of Leadership." *Training and Development Journal* 23(5): 26–34.

Mele, Nicco. 2013. *The End of Big: How the Internet Makes David the New Goliath*. New York: St. Martin's.

Nahavandi, Afsaneh. 2015. *The Art and Science of Leadership*, 7th ed. Boston: Pearson.

Sinek, Simon. 2014. *Leaders Eat Last*. New York: Penguin.

Snook, Scott A. 2008. *Leader(ship) Development*. Boston: Harvard Business School Case 408–064.

Stogdill, Ralph M. 1948. "Personal Factors Associated with Leadership: A Survey of the Literature." *Journal of Psychology* 25(1): 35–71.

CARMEN WERDER directs the Learning Commons at Western Washington University, including the Teaching-Learning Academy. She was a 2005 Carnegie Scholar and is co-editor and contributing author of Engaging Students in the Study of Teaching and Learning.

JOSEPH GARCIA is the founding and former director of the Karen W. Morse Institute for Leadership at Western Washington University. He recently completed a term as the Bowman Distinguished Professor of Leadership Studies and is currently Professor of Management in the College of Business and Economics, Western Washington University.

JAMIE BUSH is a senior at Western Washington University, majoring in English literature and minoring in writing studies. She actively participates in the Teaching-Learning Academy, and writes for a growing club on campus called Middle Women.

CAROLINE DALLSTREAM is a senior in the Honors Program at Western Washington University, majoring in environmental studies and minoring in leadership studies. She works with the Teaching-Learning Academy, the Academic Advising Center, and the Outdoor Center.

7

This chapter describes four new leadership areas in the development of faculty learning community programs and provides perspectives and resources that these leaders can use to engage their work.

Four Positions of Leadership in Planning, Implementing, and Sustaining Faculty Learning Community Programs

Milton D. Cox

One of the important collaborative structures in higher education established during the last 35 years is the faculty learning community (FLC).

> Higher education has been very slow to embrace the fact that knowing, teaching, and learning are communal enterprises, and to reflect that reality in the way it pursues its mission. But the pace of change has been picking up over the past two decades, and the learning communities movement has been at the forefront of that quickening (personal communication, Parker J. Palmer, August 18, 2010).

Leadership in FLCs has not been given much attention in the literature. Starting with its first issue in 2009, the *Learning Communities Journal* has published 43 articles about student and faculty learning communities and communities of practice. A search for the word *leadership* throughout these article titles and abstracts, in the time frame of 2009–2014, yielded only two articles: one about student learning communities and the other about communities of practice (CoPs). A similar search for the word *leader* identified three articles, two about student learning communities and one about FLCs. The abstract for the article about FLCs includes, "Just as faculty learning communities differ qualitatively from other familiar work groups in higher education, the role of the facilitator differs from what are perhaps more familiar roles of content expert, lecturer, chairperson, or traditional leader" (Ortquist-Ahrens and Toroysan 2009, p. 29). According to Bens (2000, p. 7), "[f]acilitation is a way of providing leadership without taking the reins. As a facilitator, your job is to get others to assume responsibility and take the lead." Therein may be an explanation for the absence of discussion about leadership with respect to FLCs.

During the first decade of U.S. national FLC dissemination, 2001–2010, developers were concerned that FLC facilitators might behave as directive leaders in working with their FLC members; hence, developers downplayed the use of *leadership* and *leader.* In the book, *Building Faculty Learning Communities* (Cox and Richlin 2004), Petrone and Ortquist-Ahrens (2004) share an imagined dialogue that a faculty developer who was experienced with FLCs might have with a new developer.

> Why do you use the term "facilitator" rather than "leader"?
>
> Although unique in their structure and desired outcomes, FLCs require the same task- and team-building guidance as any other work group. In the course of a semester or academic year, the FLC facilitator will function in a non-linear way in three main roles—those of champion, coordinator, and energizer. However, unlike the goal of a traditional group leader, the ultimate goal of the facilitator is not to maintain the leadership position but to help move the members of the FLC to the point where they gradually assume these roles themselves (Petrone and Ortquist-Ahrens 2004, p. 64).

Today in FLC development, the difference between leading and facilitating an FLC is well known with respect to the time period during which the FLC is holding its meetings, and the literature is generous on the topic of facilitating FLC sessions. In this chapter, we will examine the less-known role of leadership in the broader institutional structure involving FLCs. We will describe four roles that leaders, not facilitators, play in the overall FLC construct. These roles are (1) "Investigator," who is interested in learning about FLCs and leads the efforts to bring related information to the institution; (2) "Implementer," who leads efforts on campus to establish FLCs as effective and sustainable faculty development approaches; (3) "FLC Program Director," who, once a system of FLCs is established, organizes, advises, energizes, champions, and supports the FLCs in place at the institution; and (4) "FLC Prefacilitator" of a specific FLC during the time before meeting with the FLC members—namely, when contemplating, planning, proposing, recruiting, and securing local support for the specific FLC. One or more persons can hold each of these four positions, and the same person may fill two or more of the four roles.

Faculty Learning Communities

Before addressing the four FLC leadership roles just mentioned, here is a brief review of the FLC concept. In 1979, Miami University established FLCs to address the pedagogical underpreparation of early-career academics. During the period from 1974 to 1988, universities in the United

States focused their expectations, development, and rewards on the task of establishing junior faculty as producers of disciplinary discovery scholarship. Most universities paid little attention to pedagogy during this time. To address this shortcoming, the Lilly Endowment, a private foundation, awarded three-year grants to invited universities, encouraging them to design their own pedagogical development programs for early-career academics (Austin 1992; Cox 1994, 1995). The structure and process that Miami University designed and implemented defined the FLC model whose members were called teaching scholars. The name faculty learning community was not originated until the late 1990s at Miami University.

This new, small-group model of early-career faculty teaching development incorporated goals and operating procedures to address certain worrisome long-term shortcomings in U.S. higher education. Dewey (1933) expressed concern about the lack of active, student-centered, inquiry-based learning. Meanwhile, increasing specialization motivated Meiklejohn (1932) to call for a unity and coherence of curricula across disciplines. Both educators independently proposed a new curriculum and learning model, now called a student learning community (SLC), as a venue to address these shortcomings. Research conducted in the 1990s on student engagement and learning in SLCs showed that when compared with students not in SLCs, SLC students had a higher institutional retention rate, faster cognitive-structural intellectual development, and a higher level of civic engagement (MacGregor, Tinto, and Lindblad 2001). Research on the Miami University faculty small-group approach during the 1980s and 1990s confirmed similar outcomes for early-career academic participants; for example, higher tenure rates (retention) for those in the program (Cox 1995). Hence, these faculty small groups were then called faculty learning communities.

Developed in 1979, independently of SLCs, a "*faculty learning community* (FLC) is a voluntary, structured, year-long, multi-disciplinary, community of practice of around 6–12 participants (8–10 is ideal) that includes building community and the development of scholarly teaching and the scholarship of teaching and learning" (Cox, Richlin, and Essington 2014, p. 1.5). There are two types of FLCs: *cohort-based* and *topic-based*. Cohort-based FLCs address the teaching, learning, and developmental needs of a certain cohort of academics. The curriculum is shaped by the participants to include a broad range of teaching, learning, and institutional areas and topics of interest to them. These FLCs can make a positive impact on the culture of the institution over the years if given multiyear support (Cox 2006). Examples of cohort-based FLCs include early-career academics (the original FLC model now in its 37th year at Miami University) (Cox 2013), senior and midcareer academics, part-time and adjunct faculty, department chairs, lecturers and clinical faculty, and women associate professors.

A topic-based FLC has a curriculum, designed by participants, to address a special campus teaching and learning challenge or opportunity; for example, developing electronic portfolios, designing and implementing a course or curriculum on ecological sustainability, using mobile technology in courses, or team-based learning. These FLCs offer membership and provide opportunities for learning and the scholarship of teaching and learning across all academic ranks and cohorts with a focus on the particular topic (Cox 2004).

FLCs have evolved in four phases: one-dimensional, cohort development for junior faculty, 1978–1988, at Miami University (Cox 1994, 1995); local multidimensionality—the broadening of the model from the junior faculty cohort FLC to other cohorts and topic-based FLCs at Miami University, 1989–1998 (Cox 2001); extension of the model to the state of Ohio and U. S. with assessment of the model in multiple venues, 1999–2008 (Beach and Cox 2009; Cox 2006; Cox and Richlin 2004); and international extension of the model, 2009-present (Kwong et al. 2016; Wong et al. 2016).

The peak of FLC programming at Miami University occurred in 2008–2009 when the teaching and learning center managed 18 FLCs involving 17 percent of the full-time faculty. At that point in time, 52 percent of the full-time faculty and 54 percent of department chairs had participated in an FLC. Since 1990, there have been 169 FLCs at Miami University, with 46 of them cohort-based and 123 topic-based. This widespread engagement offers the university the potential of becoming a learning organization, one that connects its members closely to the mission, goals, and challenges of the institution, thus enabling it to meet the demands of change (Cox 2001; Haynes et al. 2010; Senge 1990).

When the number of FLCs offered and run by a center increases beyond one or two, an organizational structure should be put in place to manage the system of FLCs. This system is defined as an FLC program and, as noted earlier, the leader is called the FLC program director. Needless to say, when Miami University's center had 18 FLCs running, this management system and director were key to having efficient and productive FLC outcomes. We will speak more about this later.

Outcomes based on research involved with the FLC movement have identified the following beneficial results in educational development programming:

1. FLCs provide an effective platform for working with academics to develop the scholarship of teaching and learning (SoTL) (Beach and Cox 2009; Cox 2003).
2. Applying the outcomes of implementation science (Fixsen et al. 2005), FLCs provide the most effective educational development programming model for implementing evidence-based interventions (Cox 2014).
3. Early-career faculty who participate in cohort FLCs for early-career faculty at Miami University have been tenured at a significantly higher rate than those who do not (Cox 1995).

4. Academics in FLCs report the following top-five impacts that FLC participation has had on their development (Beach and Cox 2009):
   a. Perspective of teaching, learning, and higher education beyond their own disciplines.
   b. Interest in the teaching process.
   c. Understanding of and interest in SoTL.
   d. View of teaching as an intellectual pursuit.
   e. Comfort level as a member of the university community.
5. Academics in FLCs report that the top-ten impacts on their students' learning as a result of their FLC participation are all high on the Bloom taxonomy (Beach and Cox 2009).
6. FLC participants, when asked how they accomplished the changes in student learning that they reported in point 5, cited these five teaching and learning approaches as the top five (Beach and Cox 2009):
   a. Active learning.
   b. Student-centered learning.
   c. Discussion.
   d. Cooperative or collaborative learning.
   e. Writing.

To conclude this overview of FLCs, note the following structural items: an FLC is not a committee, task force, course, book club, or action learning set. These structures may lack community or the scholarship of teaching and learning development. An FLC is a small-group learning structure with a process that enables its participants to investigate and provide solutions for any significant problem or opportunity in higher education.

The following four sections are descriptions of each of the four new roles of leadership related to FLCs.

The Investigator

The person on campus responsible for raising interest in FLCs and leading the planning for investigation of them is the "FLC investigator." Institutions interested in investigating FLCs as potential resources have some options to consider., For example, they may examine the FLC literature or host on- and/or off-campus FLC workshops led by colleagues experienced with FLCs. The FLC investigator may be a member of a teaching and learning center (hereafter "center") that is considering the addition of FLCs to its faculty/educational development programming. If the institution has no center, as is sometimes the case at a small college, the FLC investigator may be a faculty member or administrator who has heard about the positive outcomes of FLCs. This person assumes a leadership role of "investigator" to learn about FLCs and bring information back to campus.

With respect to participation in an off-campus FLC all-day workshop or up to a 3.5-day FLC institute, the FLC investigator should journey with a campus team of at least an additional colleague in order to have, upon return, mutual support for advocating for and informing about FLCs. An example of programming for a one-day FLC workshop (Exhibit 1), led by experienced FLC colleagues, can be found in Miami University's Scholarly Commons, at: https://sc.lib.miamioh.edu/handle/2374.MIA/5829. Another approach that the investigator can engage is to invite an FLC expert to campus to present sessions and consult about FLCs. The visits can vary in length. For example, a two-hour workshop can provide a basic introduction to FLCs when the institution is somewhat familiar with FLCs and the center is reintroducing, renewing, or remaking the FLC program. A half-day workshop can deliver a similar program. For an institution that is considering FLCs for the first time, a one- or two-day workshop is appropriate. This may be held during a faculty all-day retreat at the start of the academic year or anytime for a small group of faculty, administrators, and center staff who are planning to implement an FLC program. Examples of such workshops are available from the author and can be tailored for an institution's culture, goals, and objectives.

A leadership plan for the FLC investigator should include meeting with stakeholders on campus to decide which investigative approach works for the institution and what questions to pursue with FLC experts. If traveling to an external workshop or institute, the investigator should select a team that will represent different areas of the institution and will be able to effectively disseminate what was learned about FLCs.

In 2015, the facilitators of a one-day FLC workshop (Exhibit 1, in Miami University's Scholarly Commons, at: https://sc.lib.miamioh.edu/handle/2374.MIA/5829), with 21 people, e-mailed a pre-workshop survey to each participant for electronic return before the workshop began. One question asked each respondent to indicate what FLC roles they are interested in—what they were seeking at the workshop as FLC investigators. Facilitating an FLC was selected by 33 percent, becoming an FLC program director by 18 percent, participating in an FLC by 21 percent, and working at the institution as an FLC implementer by 27 percent. These percentages confirm that although the leadership role of FLC implementer is newly labelled, the tasks that await an implementer back on the home campus are known. The percentages also confirm that the role of FLC facilitator is well known, whereas the FLC program director, a leadership position first noted in 2012 (Cox, Richlin, and Essington 2014), is not well known or much in use.

The Implementer

If the FLC investigator finds positive information about FLCs to share with the institution, then the implementation of an FLC program is the next step. FLC workshop facilitators find that *a good fit between the institution and the FLC model* means that adapting the model to the culture and the needs of the institution has potential. Inspiring a core of faculty supporters is a must, but the value of securing acceptance, endorsement, and support from the administration depends on the nature of faculty-administrative relationships. Of course, the ideal connection is one that is supportive in each direction.

The leadership qualities needed for the implementer are different from those of the investigator. The investigator should be a good detective who knows organizational development and the culture and needs of the institution; he or she should be familiar with faculty development issues and opportunities. The FLC implementer should be well-known, respected, and trusted around the institution. He or she should be a well-organized planner, teacher, mentor, and learner who has the ability to convince colleagues of worthwhile innovations to pursue. The implementer already may be the director of the center, the person who served as the FLC investigator, or the leader of a team that has decided to initiate the FLC effort.

In 2012, FLC developers Cox, Richlin, and Essington (2014) designed a Preliminary Planning Inventory (the "Inventory") to guide the FLC implementer through a selection of various options involving the design of an FLC and FLC Program. This inventory is a 12-point decision-making process that begins as part of an FLC workshop. Materials, training, and consultation received at the workshop equip the FLC investigator to prepare the FLC implementer for a design and initiation process for the FLC program. If at all possible, both should attend FLC workshops. Each of the 12 decision points engages a sequence of questions that prompt the implementer and planners to explore a variety of options that can affect accomplishment of the goals, objectives, and outcomes for a specific FLC and FLC program. A first task for the FLC implementer is to plan the implementation process with the center director and staff. Working through the inventory provides an excellent opportunity for designing and implementing an FLC and FLC program. The FLC Preliminary Planning Inventory (Exhibit 2) is available in Miami University's Scholarly Commons: https://sc.lib.miamioh.edu/handle/2374.MIA/5829. After working through the inventory and designing FLCs and the FLC program, the implementer and planners will need to select a way to introduce FLCs to the campus. Several approaches are available; for example, a center can invite FLC-experts to visit campus and offer workshops, consult with potential FLC facilitators, and be available for consultation as the first FLC year unfolds. Only one FLC might begin during the first year because the center wishes to take a cautious approach to hosting its first FLC.

There are examples of distinctive approaches that have been successful in implementing FLC programs. Xavier University in Cincinnati decided that it would start a center and an FLC program at the same time; the successes of both initiatives were intertwined, illustrating how effectively FLCs can enhance teaching, learning, and faculty development. Ohio University began its first year with an FLC about planning and facilitating FLCs.

Each member applied to be in this first FLC by proposing to spend the year planning, advertising, and finding membership for his or her FLC in the following year; working together was a big advantage for the FLC planners. Indiana University Southeast started with an all-day faculty retreat in which the morning involved learning about FLCs, and in the afternoon, six faculty members, whom the center invited, each led three consecutive 30-minute sessions on a topic they would pursue if they were facilitating an FLC. Faculty members at the retreat visited three topics of interest to them and decided whether they would like to be in one of those FLCs, if offered.

In summary, the FLC implementer oversees the FLC design and installation, hence setting the future of the FLC program, the commitment of its participants, and the outcomes of many of the Center's efforts. However, now that FLCs have been implemented, a leadership position is needed to sustain the FLC program.

The Program Director

The FLC program director is typically a center staff member who works with the FLCs, their facilitators, and other staff of the center. The program director oversees the year-long evolution of each of the center's FLCs, from the application that a faculty member submits to the center for facilitating an FLC through the presentation of the FLC's outcomes and graduation of its members. The program director coordinates various center staff members to enable each FLC facilitator to concentrate on his or her main tasks, namely building community in the FLC, providing an evidence- and project-based approach to the scholarship of teaching and learning, maintaining member commitment, and enjoying the process him/herself or ensuring that members enjoy the process. To make these things happen, the program director must coordinate connections that will enable FLC websites, monitor and balance budgets, order food, schedule rooms, arrange travel, and distribute and collect assessment material for all FLCs. The FLC program director is there to serve the FLC facilitators and the center staff.

Consultation plays a big part in the job, for example, such as in working with the center director to communicate latest budget developments to facilitators or supplying a report that an administrator is requesting. The FLC program director works with colleagues who are new to the institution and curious about FLCs, with facilitators who want to have their FLCs meet together, and with those who would like to add an additional term to their FLC (which usually does not result).

The FLC program director may serve as ombudsperson to address a prickly situation in an FLC, may have to nudge facilitators whose FLCs are behind in submitting FLC assessment data, and may have to consult with a facilitator whose FLC members report they are in the storming stage of small group development (Tuckman and Jensen 1977). The FLC program director is a collaborator with the FLCs and their facilitators in the FLC program, not a micromanager or inspector. As a program director, the author was invited to meetings of various FLCs to hear a member's presentation, provide insights about how to initiate proposals for project presentations, and to enjoy a meal with colleagues.

The long-term goal of the FLC program director is to sustain an effective FLC program, while remaining faithful to the FLC model. Based on research about and experience with FLCs, in 2013, Cox made 16 recommendations for sustaining an effective FLC program (Cox, Richlin, and Essignton 2014). The size of the FLC program—two or 18 or an intermediate number of FLCs—will determine the method of the program's operation, resources, and complexity, but the 16 recommendations should be followed or adapted to the culture and goals of the institution. These 16 recommendations are given in Exhibit 3 (see Figure 7.1).

The FLC Prefacilitator

Facilitating an FLC—the gentle dynamics of working with small groups and the related academic challenges of developing the scholarship of teaching and learning that is often a new scholarship for both FLC members and facilitators—has captured the attention of those working with FLCs over the FLC developmental years (Cox 2001; Petrone and Ortquist-Ahrens 2004; Ortquist-Ahrens and Torosyan 2009). Overlooked has been the FLC planning and organizational groundwork that the applying facilitator must accomplish before his or her specific FLC meets, and even before crafting the application to the center proposing that this FLC be offered. Because most potential FLC facilitators are not involved with the FLC investigator, implementer, or program director phases of FLC development, they may not have been exposed to the resources that these leaders were—namely, the FLC workshop material of the investigator, the 12 decision points and their related planning questions for the implementer, or the 16 recommendations (Exhibit 3) for the program director. Thus the FLC prefacilitator, before he or she begins facilitating the very first FLC meeting, has much to learn about FLCs. This point before facilitating the FLC is the prefacilitator stage, when he or she is in a leadership role as a planner, applicant, advocate, and recruiter for his or her specific FLC.

One point of assistance is to make these resources available to all interested in facilitating an FLC. However, reading the materials does not provide the rich discussions that the investigators have had in the workshops or the implementers have had at their planning meetings. Thus, before a potential facilitator of a specific FLC begins his or her role as facilitator in FLC meetings, that person must be a leader, not facilitator—a planner, a designer, an advocate, a recruiter—investing in leadership time before facilitating, performing leadership functions while being prefacilitator. Consultation with and support from the FLC program director can provide this and is an important task of the program director, who may gather potential facilitators to provide the discussions that repeat those from the workshops that the investigator experienced and the planning meetings that the implementer engaged.

Figure 7.1. Sixteen Recommendations for Creating and Sustaining Effective FLCs

1. Limit your FLC to a workable size: 8 to 10 (6–12 perhaps) faculty, professionals, and administrators.

2. Make membership voluntary and use an application process with department chair sign off.

3. Consider having affiliate partners: mentors, student associates, consultants.

4. Select a multidisciplinary FLC cohort, topic, goals, and membership; 3 reasons: participant curiosity, rich innovations, dysfunctional unit relief

5. Meet every 3 weeks for 2 hours for one academic year, and determine meeting time at the point of member applications.

6. Provide social moments, community, and food at meetings; an FLC is not just a committee or task force.

7. Make the facilitator a key participating member who models desired behavior and initially determines goals.

8. Have members determine FLC objectives, meeting topics, budget.

9. Focus on obtaining and maintaining FLC member commitment.

10. Assess 3 areas of FLC impact: member development, student learning or effectiveness of innovation, and FLC components engaged.

11. Employ an evidenced-based, scholarly approach leading to SoTL.

12. Present the FLC outcomes to the campus and at conferences.

13. Blend online/distance FLCs with an initial and 2 or 3 face-to-face meetings when possible.

14. Include enablers such as rewards, recognition, and a celebratory ending.

15. Imbed an FLC Program into a Teaching and Learning Center and have an FLC Program Director.

16. *Adapt* the FLC model for your readiness and institutional culture.

Conclusion

This chapter has addressed the missing context of leadership in the FLC movement. The four FLC leadership positions described here, along with the three resources included that enable each leadership opportunity to succeed, will explain and shore up some of the weaknesses that have been encountered with respect to the FLC educational development experience. refers to the "New and Experienced FLC Developer's One-Day Workshop" and Exhibit 2 features the "Preliminary Planning Inventory" [Exhibits 1 and 2 are available in the Miami University's Scholarly Commons: https://sc.lib.miamioh.edu/handle/2374.MIA/5829]. Exhibit 3 discusses Sixteen Recommendations for Creating and Sustaining Effective FLCs and is included in this chapter as Figure 7.1. These references will prove invaluable in overcoming these perceived weaknesses.

For example, one FLC weakness that has been occasionally reported is the difficulty, in some cases, of keeping FLC participant commitment active over the entire year of the FLC. Without these recognized leadership positions, the facilitator experiencing a lack of commitment may have no one to consult. If there is an FLC program director, he or she will have had training that includes use of recommendation 9, obtaining and maintaining commitment. Alternatively, the implementer or investigator will have worked through decision point 7, and hence be able to apply development of community to build commitment.

With these well-organized FLC leadership positions, FLC efforts can become professional and a key part of a professional teaching and learning center. Colleges and universities with new or established centers have exciting opportunities to enhance teaching and learning on their campuses by involving FLCs. The structural, organizational, and leadership approach of "building by FLCs" is a plan and process that can and does work well in higher education.

References

Austin, Ann E. 1992. "Supporting Junior Faculty Through a Teaching Fellows Program." In *Developing New and Junior Faculty*, New Directions for Teaching and Learning, no. 50, edited by Mary Deane Sorcinelli and Ann E. Austin, 73–86. San Francisco: Jossey-Bass.

Beach, Andrea L., and Milton D. Cox. 2009. "The Impact of Faculty Learning Communities on Teaching and Learning." *Learning Communities Journal* 1(1): 7–27.

Bens, Ingrid. 2000. *Facilitating with Ease! A Step-by-Step Guidebook*. San Francisco: Jossey-Bass.

Cox, Milton D. 1994. "Reclaiming Teaching Excellence: Miami University's Teaching Scholars Program." *To Improve the Academy* 13: 79–96.

Cox, Milton D. 1995. "The Development of New and Junior Faculty." In *Teaching Improvement Practices: Successful Strategies for Higher Education*, edited by W. Alan Wright and Associates. Bolton, MA: Anker.

Cox, Milton D. 2001. "Faculty Learning Communities: Change Agents for Transforming Institutions into Learning Organizations." *To Improve the Academy* 19: 69–93.

Cox, Milton D. 2003. "Fostering the Scholarship of Teaching through Faculty Learning Communities." *Journal on Excellence in College Teaching* 14(2/3): 161–198.

Cox, Milton D. 2004. "Introduction to Faculty Learning Communities." In *Building Faculty Learning Communities*, New Directions for Teaching and Learning, no. 97, edited by Milton D. Cox and Laurie Richlin, 5–23. San Francisco: Jossey-Bass.

Cox, Milton D. 2006. "Phases in the Development of a Change Model: Communities of Practice as Change Agents in Higher Education." In *The Realities of Educational Change: Interventions to Promote Learning and Teaching in Higher Education*, edited by Adrian Bromage, Lynne Hunt, and Bland Tomkinson. Oxford, UK: Rutledge.

Cox, Milton D. 2013. "The Impact of Communities of Practice in Support of Early-career Academics." *International Journal for Academic Development* 18(1): 18–30.

Cox, Milton. D. 2014. "Foreword." In *Inquiry-Based Learning for Faculty and Institutional Development*. Innovations in Higher Education Teaching and Learning, Volume 1, edited by Patrick Blessinger and John M. Carfora. Bingley, UK: Emerald.

Cox, Milton D., and Laurie Richlin, eds. 2004. *Building Faculty Learning Communities*. New Directions for Teaching and Learning, no. 97. San Francisco: Jossey-Bass.

Cox, Milton D., Laurie Richlin, and Amy Essington. 2014. *Faculty Learning Community Planning Guide*. Los Angeles, CA: Alliance Publishers.

Dewey, John. 1933. *How We Think*. Lexington, MA: Heath.

Fixsen, Dean L., Sandra F. Naoom, Karen A. Blase, Robert M. Friedman, and Frances Wallace. 2005. *Implementation Research: A Synthesis of the Literature*. Tampa, FL: University of South Florida, Louis de la Parte Florida Mental Health Institute, National Implementation Research Network. (FMHI Publication #231).

Haynes, Carolyn, Hays Cummins, Madelyn Detloff, Linda Dixon, Kim Ernsting, and Ann Fuehrer. 2010. "Learning Communities and Institutional Transformation." *Learning Communities Journal* 2(2): 149–167.

Kwong, Theresa, Milton D. Cox, King Chong, Stacey Nie, and Eva Wong. 2016. "Assessing the Effect of Communities of Practice in Higher Education: The Case at Hong Kong Baptist University." *Learning Communities Journal* 8(2): 171–198.

MacGregor, Jean, Vincent Tinto, and Jerri Holland Lindblad. 2001. "Assessment of Innovative Efforts: Lessons from the Learning Community Movement." In *Assessment to Promote Deep Learning: Insight from AAHE's 2000 and 1999 Assessment Conferences*, edited by Linda Suskie. Washington, DC: AAHE.

Meiklejohn, Alexander. 1932. *The Experimental College*. New York: HarperCollins.

Ortquist-Ahrens, Leslie, and Roben Torosyan. 2009. "The Role of the Facilitator in Faculty Learning Communities: Paving the Way for Growth, Productivity, and Collegiality." *Learning Communities Journal* 1(1): 29–62.

Petrone, Martha C., and Leslie Ortquist-Ahrens. 2004. "Facilitating Faculty Learning Communities: A Compact Guide to Creating Change and Inspiring Community." In *Building Faculty Learning Communities*, New Directions for Teaching and Learning, no. 97, edited by Milton D. Cox and Laurie Richlin, pp. 137–148. San Francisco: Jossey-Bass.

Senge, Peter M. 1990. *The Fifth Discipline*. New York: Doubleday.

Tuckman, Bruce W., and Mary Ann C. Jensen. 1977. "Stages of Small Group Development." *Group and Organizational Studies* 2: 419–427.

Wong, Eva, Milton D. Cox, Theresa Kwong, Roger Fung, Peter Lau, Atara Sivan, and Vicky Chiu-wan Tam. 2016. "Establishing Communities of Practice to Enhance Teaching and Learning: The Case at Hong Kong Baptist University." *Learning Communities Journal* 8(2): 9–26.

MILTON D. COX of Miami University is founder and editor-in-chief of the Journal on Excellence in College Teaching *and the* Learning Communities Journal *and founder and director of the Original Lilly Conference on College Teaching.*

8

This chapter highlights central themes from the volume and suggests that collaboration—in the classroom, in the community, in a graduate program, or instituted across an entire campus—is an effective method to move our collective teaching and learning efforts forward.

Concluding Comments

Jeffrey L. Bernstein, Brooke A. Flinders

As we close the volume and finish our jobs as co-editors, it is striking to think about the process of which we have been a part. We convened a diverse group of educators and leaders from across the country, who had very little in common besides their knowledge about the theoretical foundations of teaching and learning and a firm belief in the power of collaboration. This process of writing and editing together and the dialogue that has occurred over the past year have resulted in an exemplar case of what is possible through collaboration.

Although applied in a wide range of settings and to varying degrees, the central themes of this volume are the importance of collaborative frameworks and the need for ongoing dialogue about teaching and learning. This final chapter begins by suggesting "next steps" for higher education as a whole (the "what" to do). It concludes by offering five essential ideas to keep in mind, moving forward, as we more intentionally design our collaborative structures (the "how" to do it).

Next Steps: What to Do

In response to the critical lessons that have been presented in this volume, we conclude by discussing the next steps we might undertake to ensure that these collaborative structures can not only be built, but that they can thrive. We borrow language from Constance Cook, a political scientist who retired as executive director of the Center for Research on Learning and Teaching at the University of Michigan. Cook (2011) states that as a teaching-center director, she "consider(s) (her)self the chief lobbyist on campus for teaching improvement (p. 19)." Dedicated and engaged teachers must do the same—when we know the value of collaborative structures (or any other teaching innovations, for that matter), we must go public in our advocacy of those strategies.

One place to concentrate our collective attention is at the institutional level, with regard to the creation of supportive structures and processes. We must advocate for our schools to develop policies that are more conducive to team-teaching, or even to co-teaching with students. Although there are certainly limits that would need to be put in place, faculty who team up to teach a single course should each be given credit for that course; otherwise, entering into a collaborative-teaching arrangement becomes prohibitive in terms of faculty workload, and few such partnerships will be forged. Making funds available or allowing other compensatory methods to support students in their collaborative work, whether inside or outside the classroom (such as through the awarding of academic credit), is vital; our own faculty–student collaborations have been greatly enhanced by our ability to compensate our students in some manner. This does not require a grant or large-scale agenda. In our experience, providing lunch to our students during a working meeting, for instance, goes a long way!

Beyond institutional structures and processes, changing the underlying culture of teaching on our campuses is perhaps even more important. We return to Randy Bass's admonition about the need to encourage the problematization of teaching. Just as departments routinely hold research colloquia, we encourage departments to hold similar sessions devoted to teaching issues. When faculty can openly discuss what is and is not working in their teaching, we open the door to important conversations about teaching and learning. Struggles in teaching become something that we are no longer forced to hide, but instead are seen as challenges that we can work together to overcome. Changing the culture requires leaders who are willing to put themselves out there, acknowledge difficulty in their own work, and seek help from others. Once these conversations begin, we are convinced they will continue of their own volition. Even the most research-driven faculty member does not want to bomb in the classroom. If institutional cultures encourage collaboration as a tool for improving teaching, and set up places and times where this can happen, good things will surely result.

A third thing we need to do is to seek out partners with whom to collaborate and, ideally, with whom to build our supporting structures. Students, of course, represent one very important set of partners with whom faculty can work—after all, who better to talk about student learning with than students? But we must also find ways to reach out to our colleagues. Milt Cox's work on Faculty Learning Communities, and the Teaching-Learning Academy at Western Washington University that Carmen Werder directs, are two inspiring examples. Whereas Cox's model provides a way to bring diverse faculty members into collaboration, Werder's example introduces students and community members into the mix. However we choose to set up these arrangements, our work will only be enhanced when we reach beyond our familiar networks and find new people with whom to work.

Finally, we return to the ideas about the scholarship of teaching and learning and our role as advocates (lobbyists) for both. In the preceding paragraphs, we have asked our institutions to fund team-teaching arrangements, and to set up programs such as Faculty Learning Communities and Teaching-Learning Academies (to name just a couple of possible models). We have asked faculty to commit their time to becoming part of informal discussion groups on how to improve teaching (with the attendant discomfort that admitting to struggles in teaching will entail), and to fundamentally explore change in the teaching-learning relationships we have with our students. Such requests are likely to fall upon deaf ears initially, given the significant competing priorities that faculty must attend to and the low level of attention that teaching sometimes receives.

Convincing faculty that teaching matters may require "giant steps" in terms of professionalization (starting as early as graduate school), and in terms of faculty rewards; when it is made clear that faculty are expected to be effective teachers in order to receive tenure, attention to teaching will surely increase! As we engage in building collaborative structures to enhance teaching and learning on our campuses, we should feel an obligation to do so in a scholarly way. We must record what we are doing, gather data on the effectiveness of our work, and make the results of our investigations public. When we approach administrators with compelling evidence that time and money spent building, maintaining, and implementing collaborative structures is time and money well spent, our work will be supported. We must all accept for ourselves the roles of lobbyists, so that we may influence those holding the power and encourage them to steer institutional resources to support our collaborative efforts and, meanwhile, buttress the work our institutions do.

Collaborative Structures: How to Do Them

We have presented broad suggestions to set the foundation for successful collaborative work across higher education; now, the question becomes, "how do we do it?" In reviewing the key literature to which we have referred, and all the lessons learned from our co-authors in this volume, we would recommend the following shared goals as ways in which we can make our individual efforts a little more impactful.

Most of us learn best when we take an active role and when we are able to "discover and construct knowledge for ourselves" (Barr and Tagg 1995, p 4.). We have made a case, throughout this volume, that an ideal setting for active learning is within a collaborative structure. Now, we propose five Es to represent the overarching concepts that are interspersed throughout each chapter of this source book, and to serve as a guide for our collaboration efforts. By intentionally incorporating these Es into our collaborative structures, we can allow students to stretch and grow.

Exposure. Students must be exposed to new ideas, to diverse people, to ambiguity, and to situations that let them try out new skills and new roles. Exposure is more possible when there is a structure in place to encourage it. This volume has demonstrated many examples of how each author creates opportunities for exposure. For example, Bernstein's peer-mentoring structure allows students exposure to leading, following, and group dynamics—good and not so good. These team-based struggles and the students' success at moving through them will provide confidence as they enter into their professional lives and are pushed to work with diverse teams and conflicting opinions. Likewise, when Galantucci and Krcatovich worked with Bernstein as his teaching assistants, they were exposed to a world of academia they did not know, but soon felt better prepared to explore and join on their own journey into the profession. We could easily say the same thing for Otty and Milton's students, who were exposed to a broader swath of the occupational therapy field, through their courses connected by service-learning experiences.

Experience. We can create opportunities for experience at every turn. Students thrive when given a chance to lead, both inside and outside the classroom. The environment is less important than the structure—in-class experiences can be designed around delineated roles and shared tasks, which facilitate opportunities for conversation, problem solving, and ultimately confidence building. Beyond the walls of the classroom, collaborative structures can take the form of a research team or a student learning community. When students have a chance to gain experience and talk through those experiences with others, the learning is realized. Flinders and her students presented a case in which students gain experience in community engagement, research, leadership, and scholarship, all within one project. When students gain these varied experiences, they (again) build confidence and have the potential to become better nurses and better leaders, as a result.

Engagement. Students must be engaged: with the curriculum, with one another, and with faculty. We all know that being passive will not result in maximal learning. Collaborative structures can provide systems and space for students in which to become engaged. When there are peer-mentoring structures in place or leadership opportunities, students engage. When there are sustained programs, rather than one-time projects, it becomes easier for students to get involved. A prime example of engagement in this volume is the Institute Leadership experience, presented by Werder et al. Participants demonstrated engagement and deep reflection on whom they had been and who they were becoming. This collaborative structure, which stresses ongoing dialogue, allowed newly-realized leadership qualities to be better understood and reframed by students, even when the students themselves do not realize how much capital they bring to the experience.

Errors (with Low-Stakes). Creating opportunities for students to make mistakes in a safe and supportive situation, with built-in structures for "debriefing" or reflecting, has been another recurring theme of this volume. Students need to take risks in order to build confidence. They can do this with the support of peers or with faculty mentors. In order for students to feel okay about these "errors," we have to create structures that provide a safety net and situations that don't revolve around graded assessments. Students will not take chances unless trusted relationships have been developed. This was another persistent theme, woven throughout this volume. Building on Richard Gale's words, we note the discomfort and "unease" involved in entering into collaborative arrangements, for faculty and students alike. Setting up comfortable safe zones in which this work can occur will make them possible.

Evidence. As noted earlier, generating and disseminating evidence about collaborative outcomes are critical first steps for creating supportive institutional cultures and for rewarding the faculty efforts required to collaborate. On a more individual level, all the examples presented by our contributing authors show tangible experiences that students can use as evidence of their learning. Structures can be established, with a goal of allowing students to build evidence of what they've done and what they've learned. As teachers, we can do this by letting students in to collaborate with us on our scholarly endeavors. When students problem-solve with us, they feel valued and that their work is meaningful and real—they are able to successfully contribute to outcomes, which push them to reconsider what they might be capable of on their own. When we design structures that allow students to co-present or co-author, for example, or when we involve students in our meetings with community partners, they have experiences on which to draw in conversations with potential employers. They become reassured of their capabilities as they transition into their new professional positions and identities.

The Last Word

The ideas in this volume are not brand new, but we have attempted to bring them together in a new way. Concepts from guiding works, such as high-impact practices (Kuh 2008) and the well-known *Seven Principles for Good Practice in Undergraduate Education* (Chickering and Gamson 1987), for example, echo throughout each chapter. This source book is meant to instigate a new conversation; to serve as a starting point for faculty who are new to teaching and learning; to encourage seasoned faculty, not new to teaching and learning, to reconsider where we've been and where we're going; and to initiate new conversations about it all. Higher education faces many profound and serious challenges, which will prove difficult to solve on our own. Collaboration may prove the best tool we have to enable meaningful and engaging experiences for our students; we hope, by working together, we can move the conversation forward and better address these challenges that lie ahead.

References

Barr, Robert B., and John Tagg. 1995. "From Teaching to Learning: A New Paradigm for Undergraduate Education." *Change* 27(6): 12–25.

Chickering, Arthur W., and Zelda F. Gamson. 1987. "Seven Principles for Good Practice in Undergraduate Education." *AAHE Bulletin* 39(7): 3–7.

Cook, Constance E. 2011. "Leading a Teaching Center." In *Advancing the Culture of Teaching on Campus: How a Teaching Center Can Make a Difference*, edited by Constance E. Cook and Matthew Kaplan. Sterling, VA: Stylus Publishing.

Kuh, George. 2008. *High-Impact Educational Practices: What They Are, Who Has Access to Them, and Why They Matter*. Washington, DC: Association of American Colleges.

JEFFREY L. BERNSTEIN is Professor of Political Science at Eastern Michigan University. He is a 2005–2006 Carnegie Scholar, and has published numerous articles and book chapters on the scholarship of teaching and learning.

BROOKE A. FLINDERS is Associate Professor of Nursing at Miami University. She incorporates service-learning and the scholarship of teaching and learning in her community-based work with young women, in the field of teen pregnancy prevention.

INDEX

Abad, Andrew P., 25, 36
Adler, Patricia A., 66
Anderson, Rebecca S., 7
Arum, Richard, 25
Association of American Colleges and Universities (AAC&U), 39, 46
Austin, Ann E., 87

Bagg, Julianne, 9, 33, 35
Banking model, of education, 66
Barkley, Elizabeth F., 51
Barratt, Katherine, 53
Barrows, Howard S., 39
Barr, Robert B., 9, 40, 66, 99
Bass, Randy, 8, 83
Beach, Andrea L., 88, 89
Beauchamp, Catherine, 18
Bendersky, Karen, 52
Bennett, William J., 25
Bens, Ingrid, 85
Bergsma, Lynda, 51, 52
Bernstein, Jeffrey L., 8, 12, 14, 25, 26, 36, 97, 102
Bittle, Mary, 40
Blanchard, Karen, 53
Blanchard, Kenneth H., 76
Blase, Karen A., 88
Bloch-Shulman, Stephen, 28, 52
Bouck, Emily C., 53
Bovill, Catherine, 9, 28
Bowen, Glenn, 51
Bower, Benjamin C., 25, 37
Box, Sara E., 25, 37
Boyer, Ernest L., 8
Brady, Mia, 51, 52
Brail, Shauna, 52
Bransford, John D., 19
Brent, Rebecca, 27
Bringle, Robert G., 40
Brown, Ann L., 19
Bruton, Dean, 52
Building Faculty Learning Communities, 86
Bumbry, Michael, 9, 33, 35
Burke, Alison, 27
Burton, Carol, 51
Bush, Jamie, 75, 84

Callister, Lynn Clark, 43
Carlascio, Allison, 11, 40, 41, 54, 55
Carlyle, Thomas, 76
Carpenter, Dick M. II, 7
Caruso, Heather M., 27
Centralized Service Learning Model (CSLM), 54; community partner in, advocacy for, 59; development of, 55–59; leadership and interpersonal skill development in, 59–60; real-world learning experiences in, 59; and recommendations, 60–62; students' perceptions of, 59–60
Chickering, Arthur W., 101
Chiu-wan Tam, Vicky, 88
Chong, King, 88
Chrislip, David D., 83
Cocking, Rodney R., 19
Collaboration, 101; and learning opportunities, 16; as marriage of insufficiencies, 16; with undergraduates, 65–73. *See also* Peer mentors; Student/teacher collaboration; Undergraduate collaborative seminar
Collaborative Assignments and Projects, 15
Collaborative structures, five essential ideas in, 99; engagement, 100; errors, 100–101; evidence, 101; experience, 100; exposure, 99–100
Collaborative teaching, 51, 53–54; combining service learning and, 54
Constructivism, 40
Cook, Constance E., 97
Cook-Sather, Alison, 9
Cooperative learning, 15, 17
Cooper, Christopher, 51
Co-teaching, 53
Cox, Milton D., 9, 40, 85–90, 93, 96
Crawford, Lindy, 7
Crone, James A., 67
Cross, K. Patricia, 51
Cruz, Laura, 51
CSLM. *See* Centralized Service Learning Model
Cuban, Larry, 25
Culley, Aaron B., 66

Cummins, Hays, 88
Curseau, Petru L., 53

Dallstream, Caroline, 75, 84
Dameron, Matthew, 39, 49, 53
Dandy, Kristina L., 52
Daniere, Amrita, 52
Davis, Elaine Actis, 27
Davis, James R., 8
Deresiewicz, William, 25
Detloff, Madelyn, 88
DeWalt, Billie R., 21–22
DeWalt, Kathleen Musante, 21–22
Dewey, John, 10, 20, 87
Dialogue: definition of, 80; and discussion, distinction between, 80–81; and leadership education, 79–80; small-group, 81
Dixon, Linda, 88
Dominguez, Lynn A., 52
Dugan, Kimberly B., 8
Duggleby, Wendy, 40
Dunlap, Joanna C., 41

Edlich, Richard F., 66
Education, meaning of purpose in, 20–21
Elinor, Linda, 80
Ellison, Patty, 40
Elmendorf, Heidi, 19
Engaging Student Voices in the Study of Teaching and Learning, 52
Ernsting, Kim, 88
Essington, Amy, 87, 90, 93

Faculty learning community (FLC), 86–89, 98; cohort-based, 87; educational development programming, 88–89; establishment of, 86–87; evolution of, 88; FLC facilitators, 85–86; leadership in, 85–86; leadership roles, 86; FLC prefacilitator, 86, 93–94; FLC program director, 86, 88, 92–93; implementer, 86, 90–92; investigator, 86, 89–90; Preliminary Planning Inventory, 91; recommendations for creating and sustaining of, 94; recommendations for sustaining of effective FLC program, 93, 94; topic-based, 87–88
Felder, Richard M., 27
Felten, Peter, 9, 28, 33, 35, 52
Fiechtner, Susan Brown, 27
Fingerson, Laura, 66
Finley, Ashley, 46
Fishman, Rachel, 51, 52
Fixsen, Dean L., 88
Flannery, Kelly, 28, 52
FLC. *See* Faculty learning community
Fleishman, Edwin A., 76
Flinders, Brooke A., 11, 12, 14, 39, 40, 41, 49, 52–55, 97, 102
Fosnot, Catherine Twomey, 39, 40, 47
Freire, Paulo, 66
Friedman, Robert M., 88
Fuehrer, Ann, 88
Fung, Roger, 88

Galantucci, Ellen G., 65, 74
Gale, Richard A., 9, 15, 23
Gamson, Zelda F., 101
Garcia, Joseph, 75, 84
Garside, Colleen, 66
Gelmon, Sherril B., 52
Gerard, Glenna, 80
Gilb, Katelyn, 11, 40, 41, 54, 55
Ginsberg, Benjamin, 25
Glascoff, Mary A., 40–41
Godek, Lauren, 52
Good, Henry, 75
Goralnik, Lissy, 51
Graduate Seminar, 55
Gray, Tara, 8
"Great Man" leadership prototype, 76
Greenberg, Jerrold S., 40
Greene, Maxine, 16, 18, 21
Group work, 16–17, 26–27
Guskin, Alan E., 66
Gutman, Ellen E., 8, 28

Habron, Geoffrey B., 51
Halbert, Sami, 8
Hart Research Associates, 60
Hatcher, Julie A., 40
Haynes, Carolyn, 88
Heinrich,William F., 51
Hensley, Thomas R., 66
Hersey, Paul, 76
Hersh, Richard H., 25
Higher education: challenges of, 25; goals of, 16; next steps for, 97–99; service learning in, 51–52. *See also* Collaboration; specific topics

High-impact practices (HIPs), 39. *See also* Service-learning program, collaboration in
Hill, Jennifer, 9, 33, 35
HIPs. *See* High-impact practices
Hobbins-Garbett, Debra, 43
Hoel, Anne, 7
Hornsby, Karen, 9, 33, 35
Huckestein, Hailey L., 25, 26, 37
Hutchings, Pat, 8, 9

Interprofessional education, 61

Jacobson, Kinga, 52
Jensen, Mary Ann C., 92
Johnson, David W., 39, 41
Johnson, Heather L., 51
Johnson Holubec, Edythe, 39–40, 41
Johnson, Roger T., 39, 41
Johnson, Sherryl W., 53
Jones, Thomas B., 39
Jordan, Catherine, 52

Kalles, Susan, 54
Karen W. Morse Institute of Leadership, Western Washington University, 75–78
Karp, David A., 66
Kava, Katherine, 39, 49, 53
King, Alison, 53
Kolb, David A., 39
Krcatovich, Erin Marie-Sergison, 65, 74
Kuh, George, 11, 15, 17, 39, 44–46, 101
Kwong, Theresa, 88

Lau, Peter, 88
Leadership, definition of, 76
Leadership education, 75–83; collaborative leader and, 82–83; evolution of, 75–77; Karen W. Morse Institute for Leadership Studies, 77–78; leading from behind, 80–82; need for collaboration in, 77; old leadership model, 77; through dialogue, 79–80
Learner-centered concepts, 40
Learner-centered environment, creation of, 70
Learning: collaborative, 53–54, 65; cooperative, 15, 17; peer, 17–18
Learning Communities Journal, 85
Leavitt, Melissa C., 7
Letterman, Margaret R., 8
Levkoe, Charles, 52
Liberal Education and America's Promise (LEAP), 39
Lilly Endowment, 87
Lindblad, Jerri Holland, 87
Little, Amanda, 7
Long, Deborah T., 28
Ludwig-Hardman, Stacey, 41

MacGregor, Jean, 87
Major, Claire Howell, 51
Mannix, Elizabeth, 27
Manor, Christopher, 28, 52
Manzer, John P., 54
Martin, Chelsea J., 8
Mbugua, Tata, 52
McDonald, James, 52
McFadden, Anna, 51
McIntosh, Noel, 66
McNair, Tia, 46
Meiklejohn, Alexander, 87
Mele, Nicco, 77
Merrow, John, 25
Meyers, Chet, 39
Miami University, 86–88
Mihans II, Richard J., 28
Mikulic, Steven M., 25, 26, 37
Miller, Richard L., 7
Milton, Lauren, 51, 63
Munson, Lawrence S., 66

Nahavandi, Afsaneh, 76
Naoom, Sandra F., 88
Nathan, Rebekah, 25
National Survey of Student Engagement, 39
Neale, Margaret A., 27
Nicholson, Louis, 11, 40, 41, 54, 55
Nie, Stacey, 88
Nowacek, Rebecca S., 9

Oakley, Maureen, 66
O'Donnell, Ken, 44–46
Ortquist-Ahrens, Leslie, 85, 86, 93
Osterholt, Dorothy A., 53
Otis, Megan, 8, 9, 35, 45, 52
Otty, Robyn, 51, 63

Palmer, Parker J., 7, 10
Participant observation, 21–22

Partnership model for service learning, 40–41, 54, 55. *See also* Centralized Service Learning Model (CSLM); Service-learning program, collaboration in
Pedagogical solitude, 7, 9, 12
Peer learning, 17; and collaborative teaching, distinction between, 17–18
Peer mentors, 26; benefits enjoyed by, 32–34; in cajoler/nag role, 30; as cheerleader, 29–30; as crisis manager, 32; as extra set of eyes and ears, 29; as sounding board, 28–29; timely intervention by, 31–32. *See also* Student, as peer mentors in audacious course-based project
Peer-to-peer conversation, 16
Peer tutoring, 17
Perry, Randall Stewart, 40, 47
Petrone, Martha C., 86, 93
Pluut, Helen, 53
Pope-Ruark, Rebecca, 51, 52
Pratt, Maria, 9, 33, 35
Preliminary Planning Inventory, 91
Problem solving, 16
Program Archive on Sexuality, Health and Adolescence (PASHA), 40, 41

Ransbury, Paige, 51, 52
Rassuli, Ali, 54
Reciprocity, 40
Reich, Chesney, 51
Richlin, Laurie, 86, 87, 88, 90, 93
Roksa, Josipa, 25
Rosales, Cecilia, 51, 52
Ryan, Thomas G., 54

Sabo, Samantha, 51, 52
Schneider, Carol Geary, 39
Scholarship of discovery, 9
Scholarship of teaching and learning (SoTL), 9, 12, 42, 55, 66, 67, 73, 88, 93, 98
Secomb, Jacinta, 17
Seifer, Serena D., 40, 52
Selingo, Jeffrey L., 25
Seminar format, 66–67
Senge, Peter M., 88
Sergison, Erin M., 8
Service learning, 51; benefits of, 52–53; and collaborative teaching, 51, 54; definition of, 40–41; in higher education, 51–52
Service-learning program, collaboration in, 39–47; collaboration within required course, 41; evaluation of leadership team's HIPs experiences, 44–46; FOCUS Program design, 40–43; HIPs included in program, 40; implementation efforts, 40–41; partnership model for service learning, 40–41; service-learning outcomes, 43–44; undergraduate associates (UAs) and research assistants (RAs) in, 41–43
Seven Principles for Good Practice in Undergraduate Education, 101
Shah, Nina P., 40
Shulman, Lee S., 7, 8, 9, 12, 15–16, 20, 30
Sinek, Simon, 75
Sivan, Atara, 88
Snook, Scott A., 78
Space for brainstorming, 29
Speck, Bruce W., 7
Steffens, Henry, 66
Stogdill, Ralph M., 76
Student, as peer mentors in audacious course-based project, 26–35; benefits for peer mentors, 32–34; experiences of student groups, 30–32; implications of work, 34–35; overview of project and course, 26–28; role of peer mentor, 28–30
Student learning community (SLC), 87
Students: on Centralized Service Learning Model, 59–60; co-learning in learning-paradigm model, 66; as collaborators, 18, 19; as peer teachers, 17–18; and service learning, 51–53. *See also* Service learning
Student/teacher collaboration, 15–21, 98; confidence and trust in, 19–20; identity, risk, and uncertainty in, 18–19; and opportunities for scholarship, 21–22; power and agency in, 20–21
Sullivan, Theresa A., 67

Tagg, John, 9, 40, 66, 99
Teacher, role of, 18–19, 20–21
Teaching, 98; collaborative, 51, 53–54; collaborative structures in, 9–10; as communal property, 8, 12;

conversation and community role in, 7, 8; and discomfort/failure risk, 10; and learning, 16; as scholarly pursuit, 9; team-teaching models, 7–8
Teaching identity, construction of, 18
Teaching-Learning Academy (TLA), 76, 77, 79–82, 98. *See also* Leadership education
Team-teaching, benefits of, 7–8
Teamwork, 17
Teufel-Shone, Nicolette, 51, 52
Thomas, Lynn, 18
Thornam, Christine, 41
Tinto, Vincent, 87
TLA. *See* Teaching-Learning Academy
Topping, Keith J., 17
Torosyan, Roben, 85, 93
Trust, role of, in collaboration, 19–20
Tuckman, Bruce W., 92

Undergraduate collaborative seminar, 65–73; academic and professional benefits, 68–70; advantage on job market, 72–73; benefits from, 65–66; and course development, 71–72; and course management, 72; flexibility in, 70, 72; as learner-centered, 70; lessons from, 70–71; problems and strategies for structuring of, 66–67; professional impact of, 71–73; project design, 68; simulation and seminar design, 67–68
United States v. Windsor, 72

Wadkins, Theresa, 7
Walden, Ron, 7
Wallace, Frances, 88
Walsh, Brian F., 25, 37
Warg, Melissa, 51
Weller, Saranne, 9, 33, 35
Wenger, Etienne, 40, 41
Wentworth, Jay, 8
Werder, Carmen, 8, 9, 35, 45, 52, 75, 84
Western's Leadership Advantage, 77
Wilezol, David, 25
Wilson, Brent, 41
Wong, Eva, 88
Woolley, Anita Williams, 27
World Health Organization, 61
Wozniak, William, 7
Wright, Richard A., 66

Ye, Feifei, 53
Yoels, William C., 66
Yorio, Patrick L., 53

Zapien, Jill de, 51, 52

NEW DIRECTIONS FOR TEACHING AND LEARNING

ORDER FORM SUBSCRIPTION AND SINGLE ISSUES

DISCOUNTED BACK ISSUES:

Use this form to receive 20% off all back issues of *New Directions for Teaching and Learning.*
All single issues priced at **$23.20** (normally $29.00)

TITLE	ISSUE NO.	ISBN

Call 1-800-835-6770 or see mailing instructions below. When calling, mention the promotional code JBNND to receive your discount. For a complete list of issues, please visit www.wiley.com/WileyCDA/WileyTitle/productCd-TL.html

SUBSCRIPTIONS: (1 YEAR, 4 ISSUES)

☐ New Order ☐ Renewal

U.S.	☐ Individual: $89	☐ Institutional: $356
Canada/Mexico	☐ Individual: $89	☐ Institutional: $398
All Others	☐ Individual: $113	☐ Institutional: $434

Call 1-800-835-6770 or see mailing and pricing instructions below.
Online subscriptions are available at www.onlinelibrary.wiley.com

ORDER TOTALS:

Issue / Subscription Amount: $ ____________

Shipping Amount: $ ____________
(for single issues only – subscription prices include shipping)

Total Amount: $ ____________

SHIPPING CHARGES:

First Item	$6.00
Each Add'l Item	$2.00

(No sales tax for U.S. subscriptions. Canadian residents, add GST for subscription orders. Individual rate subscriptions must be paid by personal check or credit card. Individual rate subscriptions may not be resold as library copies.)

BILLING & SHIPPING INFORMATION:

☐ **PAYMENT ENCLOSED:** *(U.S. check or money order only. All payments must be in U.S. dollars.)*

☐ **CREDIT CARD:** ☐ VISA ☐ MC ☐ AMEX

Card number ______________________ Exp. Date ____________

Card Holder Name ______________________ Card Issue # ____________

Signature ______________________ Day Phone ____________

☐ **BILL ME:** *(U.S. institutional orders only. Purchase order required.)*

Purchase order # ______________________

Federal Tax ID 13559302 • GST 89102-8052

Name ______________________

Address ______________________

Phone ______________________ E-mail ______________________

Copy or detach page and send to: **John Wiley & Sons, Inc. / Jossey Bass**
PO Box 55381
Boston, MA 02205-9850

PROMO JBNND

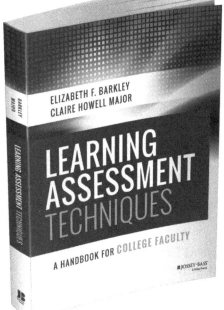

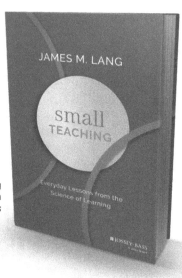

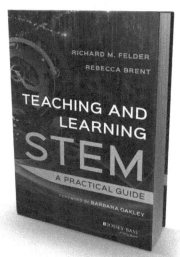